SOUTHERN · TIMES ·

Contents

Introduction	3
Some new light on the Joint LSWR / LBSCR and LSWR Steam Railmotors	5
The Southern from the Air	34
and speaking of coal……	42
Accident at Eastbourne – Buffer stop collision 23 May 1930	44
Stephen Townroe's Colour Archive	52
David McKenna. Chairman and General Manager, Southern Region 1963 – 1968	64
Off the beaten track: Southern Pacifics at Birmingham Snow Hill	68
From the archives – photo feature – EMUs	70
Guildford and Waterloo via Main Line	
A Passenger's Description of the First Electric Journeys	76
Copnor Level crossing 1908	77
Treasures from the Bluebell Railway Museum	78
From the Footplate…	80

The Transport Treasury

TIMES SERIES

Front Cover: In March 1954 S. C. Townroe recorded this stunning record of 'Merchant Navy' Pacific No 35027 *Port Line* about to leave Victoria with the down Golden Arrow pullman. This and sister No 35028 were both Stewarts Lane engines and regular performers on the train. What of course makes the image so captivating are the mother and son; the boy perhaps slightly nervous being in such close proximity to the train. Contemporary fashions of the time are another feature, the headgear especially. Somehow electric units leaving the same station nearly 70 years later do not somehow have the same appeal.

Left: Southern commercial offices at Margate. What delights in the form of ephemera might have lay hidden inside…? Rev A. Mace / Transport Treasury

Rear cover: Harking back to the article of the steam railmotors, this is a view of the up platform at Whitchurch in BR days – now Platform 1. The canopy afforded weather protection for both the up platform and what was originally the loop; the latter out of use for many years. This loop was provided for the use of the railmotor operating the Whitchurch – Fullerton service and whilst now more than a century has passed since a railmotor was seen here, it just goes to prove if you look carefully there is still evidence of and clues to past history to be found. *Bill Kellaway*

Copies of many of the images within SOUTHERN TIMES are available for purchase/download.

In addition the Transport Treasury Archive contains tens of thousands of other UK,

Irish and some European railway photographs.

© Images and design: The Transport Treasury 2022.

ISBN 978-1-913251-27-7

First Published in 2022 by Transport Treasury Publishing Ltd.,
16 Highworth Close, High Wycombe, HP13 7PJ

www.ttpublishing.co.uk *or for editorial issues and contributions email to* **southerntimes@email.com**

Printed in Tarxien, Malta by the Gutenberg Press Ltd.

INTRODUCTION

Welcome to the first issue of 'Southern Times'. It is said that a change is as good as a rest and consequently I felt it was probably time for a new approach to portraying our favourite railway.

At Transport Treasury we also have the advantage of access to their vast library of images, some 750,000 I am told (I have not counted although not all Southern related), in consequence we look forward to including examples from various collections in this and future issues.

We are also pleased to continue with some old favourites, 'The Colour Images of S. C. Townroe' being one example whilst there will also be a regular forum for letters, comments, and we hope not too many criticisms, in 'From the Footplate'.

'Southern Times' will appear for three issues in 2022 with the plan to move to quarterly publication in 2023.

Having also conducted some market research, the cover design will remain constant with Green and Cream throughout; images front and rear and of course the issue number will change each time. In this way we hope to develop a uniform style that sits pleasingly on the shelf.

Articles will continue to be as varied as possible covering the Southern and its predecessors as well as BR(S) to a realistic period. 'Blue' on occasions but we will leave the privatisation era to others far better qualified. Comment on current preservation and heritage lines will be similarly limited.

All of us who are involved, Robin, Andrew, Michelle, Laura and of course the Editor sincerely hope you enjoy both this and what is to follow. Contributions are also welcome.

We are also delighted to announce that copies of several of many of the images included in this and future issues will be available for purchase. Please contact the editorial office for further details.

Kevin Robertson

Look out for Southern Times Issue 2 in June 2022.

Content to include:

Interlude at Midhurst

The LSWR G6 0-6-0T class

More in colour from S. C. Townroe

Deptford Wharf

From the achieves: photo feature, Southern signal boxes

Southern allocations – Eastern Section 1934

Accident between Bearstead and Hollingbourne August 1927

and of course lots more!

Joint car No 1 – LBSCR livery. Although mechanically identical, the liveries of Nos 1 and 2 were different. From the outset both engine portions were painted in Drummond green, but the carriage sections differed. No 1 was in LBSCR chocolate and cream whilst No 2 carried LSWR salmon and brown. We have not located any views showing the units in their later life, whilst b/w images do not present sufficient tonal variations to confirm any subsequent changes. Lining will also be seen applied to the splashers of the wheels on the power bogie; consequently these respective liveries appear to have remained consistent throughout their short lives. Solid wheels were fitted. *Curl Collection*

Some new light on the joint LSWR / LBSCR and LSWR Steam Railmotors

The story of the various steam railmotors is one of both initiative and failure. Initiative in so far as the LSWR was one of the first British railway companies to consider the combination of a steam engine and carriage within a single vehicle and failure for perhaps not developing the idea further in later years.

Dealing with the LSWR, it cannot be said they were the very first to consider the idea of a combined unit, as back in 1848 the Bristol and Exeter Railway obtained a 'steam carriage' to the design of William Bridges Adams which was given the name *Fairfield.* Understandably it was built to run on the broad gauge. Another vehicle of like type – we hesitate to use the word 'similar' as each was to a totally different design although the concept was identical – was in use on the Enfield branch of the Eastern Counties Railway the following year, this was of course to the standard gauge. Neither appeared to have made a major impression on contemporary railway engineers of the time.

Move forward to 1873/4 and one William Robert Rowan appears on the scene with his own design of what we may now conveniently refer to as a steam railmotor. Rowan attempted to secure interest within Britain but to no avail although his patent was taken up in Austria, Switzerland and Australia. Instead, it would be technological progress in the form of the electric street tramway that would spur development and lead to steam railmotor designs intended to counter the new threat.

The Joint Committee pair: Nos 1 and 2

So far as the LSWR was concerned, it was the inauguration of an electric street tram system between Portsmouth Town station and Clarence Pier in 1901 that was the catalyst for action. Prior to this, trams had been horse drawn, but to the public the new system was seen as clean, sleek and modern (the last word perhaps slightly strange considering the designs of the time), but aesthetics apart, the result was an immediate success for the Corporation of Portsmouth and at the expense of the railway who saw receipts on the parallel East Southsea branch from Fratton drop like the proverbial stone.

To counter this threat, the joint committee that administered the line[1] approved a Dugald Drummond design of steam railmotor with two vehicles estimated to cost £1,280 ordered for the 1¼ mile branch in November 1902. Nine Elms was responsible for the boiler, mechanical fittings, wheels, frames and trailing bogie whilst Eastleigh would deal with the carriage portion. Whether any alternative options or designs were considered or submitted perhaps by the LBSCR is not reported.

According to Bradley, the first of the pair, appropriately No 1, was photographed complete outside both the Eastleigh carriage works and then Fratton station on Monday 13 April 1903 before running several trials – presumably successful - over the branch. A great pity is that it was not photographed at the East Southsea terminus which continues to remain a barren wasteland so far as images are concerned.

It was returned to Eastleigh carriage works before running overnight to Waterloo where it was inspected by officials of both the LSWR and LBSCR the next day. A demonstration run from Waterloo to Woking was planned but this had to be abandoned near to what was later the site of Hersham station, owing to overheating of the trailing bogie. Slightly strange perhaps as the vehicle had run up from Eastleigh only a few hours earlier – could the weight of passengers carried have been a consideration?

It might be expected the vehicle would have been put into service on the Southsea branch as soon as possible but instead the GWR expressed an interest and, perhaps proud to display their achievement, the LSWR loaned No 1 to the GWR for trials between Chalford and Stroud. At 1 in 70 and 1 in 75, the gradients of the Stroud Valley were far more than would be encountered on the plateau of Portsea Island and according to the *Railway Engineer* of December 1903 referring to the LSWR /LBSCR machine, '...it refused to surmount them'. Even so the concept was sufficient for the GWR and others to produce their own steam railmotors although it should be noted that the GWR cars at least had a power bogie of 0-4-0 type and were considerably more powerful compared with the small boiler and cylinders together with the single driven axle of No 1.

 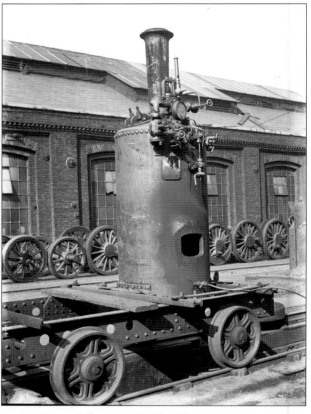

This page, left and right: The vertical boiler and firebox under construction and then outside Nine Elms shops prior to or subsequent to steam test. (The steam gauge shows zero pressure whilst on the side are the chalked words 'Light up 9'. *Curl collection*

Opposite top: Under construction within the LSWR workshops at Nine Elms. In the first view plating is being applied around the outside of the boiler; presumably with some form of insulation between the boiler sides and the casing? The necessity for outside Walschaerts valve gear is also apparent as the ash pan from the firebox is immediately above the drive axle. Note the wooden structure on top of the frames is a temporary addition to assist in placing the boiler mountings. In the same view we can clearly see what would be the hand-operated brakes working only on one side of each set of wheels.

Opposite bottom: In the second view the main frames have been added so connecting the power and carrying bogies. Possibly this was a trial fixing as the vertical boiler is not visible. Seen from this angle the impression is also almost that of the bunker of a tank engine. In this condition but with the boiler fitted, the two cars were dispatched to Eastleigh for the body of the carriage portion to be added. Unfortunately no views of the construction and fitting of the bodies have been discovered. *Curl collection*

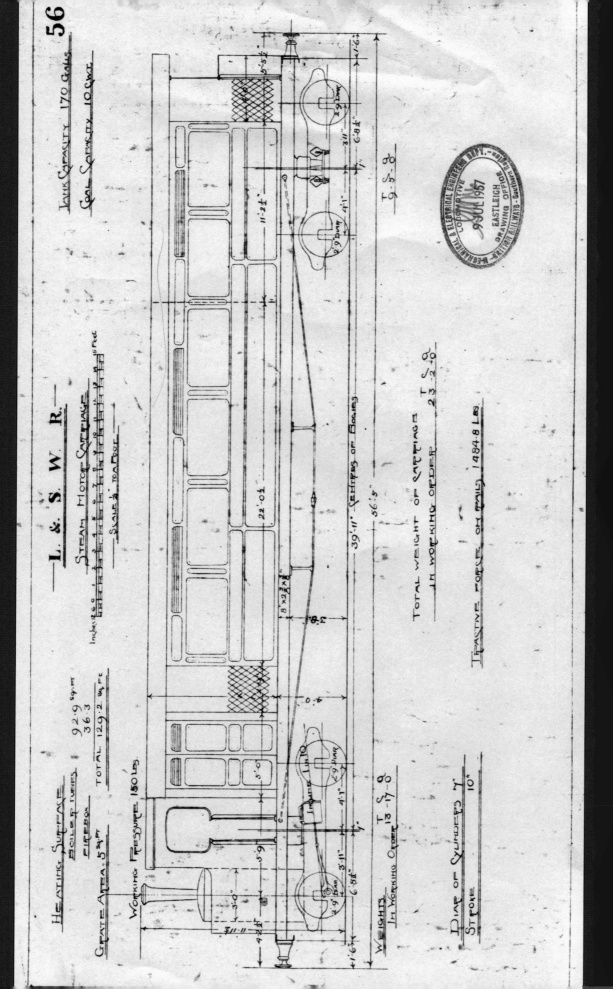

Tank Capacity 170 Galls

Coal Capacity 10 Cwt

L. & S. W. R.

Steam Motor Carriage

Scale ½ to a Foot

Heating Surface — Boiler Tubes 929 sq ft — Firebox 36·3 — Total 129·2 sq ft

Grate Area 5 sq ft

Working Pressure 150 lbs

Weight In Working Order 13 - 17 - 0

Total Weight of Carriage In Working Order 23 - 2 - 0

Tractive Force on Rails 1484·8 Lbs

Diar of Cylinders 7"

Stroke 10"

Brand new outside Eastleigh carriage and wagon works. It would be interesting to know the thoughts of the painters when instructed to prepare LBSCR livery! The polished buffer heads will also be noted. As first built the end opposite the boiler was no more than a means of access / egress for first class passengers and, as confirmed in the Board of Trade correspondence, no driving controls were fitted. *Curl collection*

The restricted performance of No 1 whilst running on GWR metals saw Drummond modify the design of the vertical boiler of No 2, then under construction, to afford an increase in steam capacity of 35%. When completed trials of both No 1 and No 2 between Cosham and Havant showed the superiority of No 2 and meaning it could accelerate to 25mph in 55 seconds, no comparative information was given for No 1. (The original design stipulation was that the car should reach 30mph from rest in 30 seconds and it is believed that this had been achieved in early tests but only by temporarily increasing the boiler pressure to 200psi.)

No 1 eventually commenced service on the Southsea branch on 1 June 1903 and was joined by No 2 soon after. Both units were stabled at the depot at Fratton. The units were kept busy with three trains per hour commencing at 7.30am and concluding at 8.00pm. There was no Sunday service.

Experience in traffic quickly showed the inability of the railcars to cope when fully laden. This normally occurred with peak morning and evening traffic, even for No 2 with its additional reserves. It thus became practice to use a conventional steam engine from Fratton, an O2 or a Terrier as a pilot. (An interesting operational conundrum as the railcars do not appear to have had a vacuum brake connection.)

Because of this poor performance, in mid-September 1903 No 1 was returned to Nine Elms for rebuilding with a larger boiler and increased cylinder diameter. The enlarged boiler was now fitted horizontally, the smokebox protruded high above the buffer beam; exactly how smokebox cleaning might have been achieved is not reported.

Changes were also made to the springing of the rear bogie to improve the ride when the carriage end was leading.

Design work on these changes must have preceded the call to works as just a short time later in October 1903 No 1 was returned to Fratton and was now found to be fully capable of the work required. No 2 was similarly modified in 1904. The original vertical boilers also found a new use, one on the steam crane at Fratton coaling stage and the other (unspecified) at Redbridge sleeper works.

From the images it may be discerned that there was little protection afforded to the 'driver' when running in reverse and it was not until 1908/9 that a full height weather board was provided with circular observation windows. It also raises the question, did the driver simply ride as an 'observer' at the front at this stage or did he remain on the footplate?

This itself raises an interesting point that appears not to have been brought up elsewhere. It appears in LSWR correspondence to the Board of Trade dated 4 February 1904,

"In reply to your letter of 27 ultimo…., I beg to inform you that the working of the steam motor service on the Fratton and East Southsea line has been quite satisfactory and no difficulty whatever has been experienced owing to the Driver being at the trailing end of the vehicle on up journeys.

"I note the statement that the Board of Trade have decided to make it a requirement for the future that such a vehicle shall be capable of being driven at either end and so that the Driver shall be always be at the front of the car…… . "

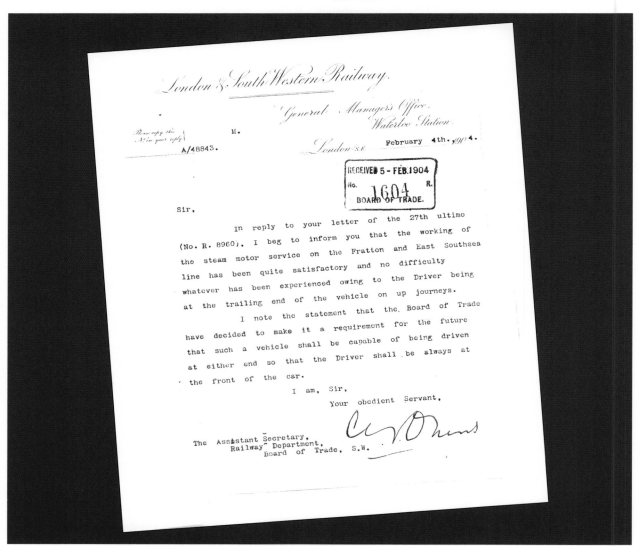

Believed to be the interior of one of the joint cars; austere yet functional for what was only a short journey. We might even ponder on the justification for a First Class saloon on the East Southsea line, after all if the railcars were intended to compete with the street trams there was no First Class on the tram service. 32 third class and 14 first class passengers could be carried, presumably the latter were provided with padded seats! *Curl collection*

This is a fascinating revelation and means that the initial services were being operated in effect as a propelling passenger train; no wonder the B. of T. were demanding change. It also goes to explain why a simple weatherboard was at first the only thing provided. Considering the date of the correspondence, 1904, it is slightly surprising to note that the full height weatherboard was not provided until some years later although presumably duplicate controls had been fitted earlier. The lesson had been learnt and driving positions were standard at both ends on subsequent designs.

Despite the presence of the railcars, the competing street tramway was still winning so far as passenger numbers were concerned with the result that by 1912 the Joint Committee were making an estimated loss of £820 annually, equivalent to over £900,000 in today's figures. It comes then as a slight surprise that new fireboxes and improved seating (padded now perhaps?) – the original seats had been of wood and comparable with a contemporary tram – were authorised for both cars in 1912/13.

The outbreak of war in August 1914 was probably taken as an excuse to terminate services on the branch; they would never resume. Both cars were then stored at the rear of Eastleigh works. In light of the joint ownership of the vehicles, No 1 was despatched to Brighton where it was initially stored for some time behind the paint shop at Preston Park in company with a number of E4 0-6-2T locos returned from ROD service in France. It was soon broken up whilst on the LSWR the engine section of No 2 was removed and the carriage portion converted into a non-powered coach for motor train operation.

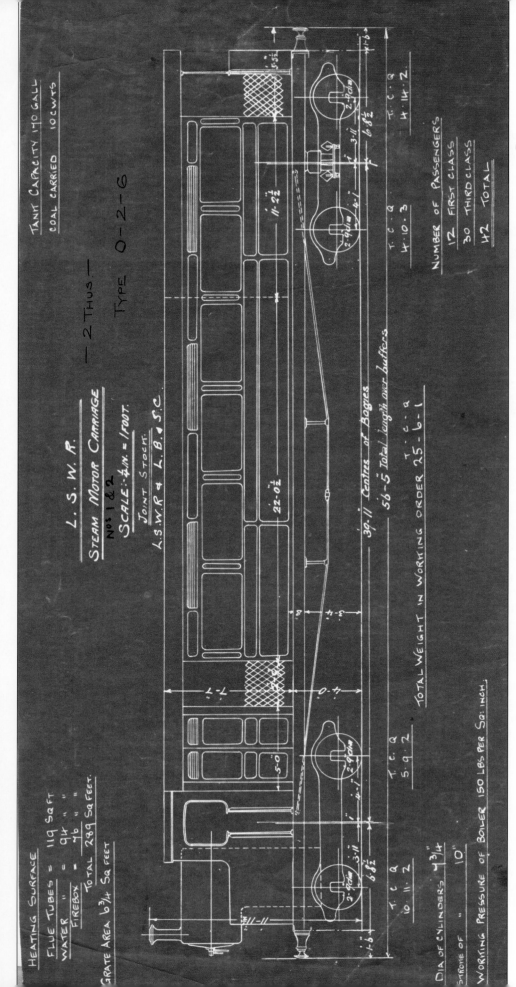

HEATING SURFACE
FLUE TUBES = 119 SQ FT
WATER " = 94 " "
FIREBOX " = 76 " "
TOTAL 289 SQ FEET.

GRATE AREA 63/4 SQ FEET

DIA OF CYLINDERS 9¾"
STROKE OF " 10"
WORKING PRESSURE OF BOILER 150 LBS PER SQ. INCH.

L.S.W.R.
STEAM MOTOR CARRIAGE
Nos 1 & 2
SCALE:-4IN.=1FOOT.
— 2 THUS.—
TYPE O-2-6

JOINT STOCK:
L.S.W.R & L.B.S.C.

TOTAL WEIGHT IN WORKING ORDER 25 - 6 - 1

TANK CAPACITY 190 GALL
COAL CARRIED 10 CWTS

NUMBER OF PASSENGERS
12 FIRST CLASS
30 THIRD CLASS
42 TOTAL

This page: Blueprint of joint cars Nos 1 and 2 as modified. The cylindrical tanks attached to the underframe carried the engine water supply. Mr T. Hurry Richards[2], Locomotive Superintendent of the Taff Vale Railway, wrote to Drummond soon after the Chalford trials asking for drawings and patterns so a more powerful car might be built. This release was approved by the LSWR Board whilst Drummond is known to have visited Cardiff during construction. The completed Taff Vale vehicle was interesting in that it had two short boilers either side of a central firebox, the engine portion also articulated from the carriage. In service it proved reasonably successful. Having proven itself the TVR design was multiplied with a further 15 examples although all had ceased work by the early 1920s. Returning to Portsmouth, and apart from the trials mentioned in the text, it is believed Nos 1 and 2 spent almost the whole of their lives on the Southsea branch. *Ian Wilkins collection*

Opposite: Joint car No 1 as modified with larger boiler and firebox and seen from both sides. It is ironic that No 2 seems to have been somewhat camera shy. The strong objections by the Board of Trade related not only to the driver's view when running in reverse but also that only a hand brake was provided and that the saloons were lit by oil. The purpose of the gauge seen on the solebar is not confirmed but it is likely it was in conjunction with the water capacity. Three crew were still required. Subsequent to the fitting of duplicate driving controls at the opposite end, electric bell communication was provided between the cabs and presumably the guard. One ton of luggage might be carried. Folklore has it a pinch bar was regularly carried as it was sometimes necessary to move the car over top dead centre. Another story relates that if the car were stopped for minor engine repairs, it might still be hauled dead to maintain services. Nos 1 and 2 worked the East Southsea service on alternate days, under normal circumstances a journey without incident taking just five minutes in either direction inclusive of stops at the two intermediate halts. Despite being fitted with conventional buffing gear, it is not believed there was ever an attempt at the hauling of a trailing load.

Nos 1 and 2 Order (Class) No K11	As built	As modified Oct 1903 (No 1), June 1904 (No 2)
Overall length	56' 8"	
Total wheelbase	47' 11"	
Bogie wheelbase	8' 9"	
Wheel diameter	2' 9"	
Cylinders 2 (outside)	7" x 10"	7¾" x 10"
Boiler diameter	3' 0"	3' 1"
Boiler length	3' 3"	3' 10"
Firebox length	2' 8"	2' 4"
Heating surface:		
Tubes	92.9 sq ft	94 sq ft
Firebox	36.3 sq ft	76 sq ft
Cross water tubes	n/a	119 sq ft
Working pressure	150 psi	150 psi
Grate area	5 sq ft	6¾ sq ft
Water capacity	170 gallons	
Coal capacity	6 cwt	
Weights in working order		
Engine bogie	13t 17cwt	16t 1cwt
Trailing bogie	9t 5cwt	10t 6cwt
Total weight	23t 2cwt	26t 7cwt
Seating capacity		
First class	12	
Third class	30	

The H12 Railmotors, Nos 1 and 2.

Despite what was really the limited success of the joint committee vehicles, Drummond was evidently satisfied enough to develop the principal further with the H12 class, a duplicate Nos 1 and 2 appearing in May and June 1904 respectively. As previous, Nine Elms was responsible for all barring the carriage body and interior.

According to Bradley, the provisions of the luggage compartment next to the engine on the joint cars had not been totally satisfactory although he does not elaborate as to the reason and we have no plan view to confirm if there had been access available by the guard to the passenger saloon whilst the railcar was on the move.

As before, the boiler and firebox were at one end of the vehicle but this time turned in to face the passenger compartment, the driver would therefore have his back to the controls when driving from this end. The accompanying drawing and photographs confirm the position of the chimney and smokebox but we have no idea how the latter might have been accessible for cleaning. Aesthetically the vehicles were not the most attractive from the side with the large expanse of sheeting at one end covering the boiler portion. As before, oil lighting and a hand brake only were provided but this was changed to electricity and vacuum as early as September 1904 and again following representations from the Board of Trade. (It is not believed this similar change was made on the joint cars.)

The H12 design was not built with the intention of competing with a tramway but instead was a serious attempt to reduce operating costs on lines where there was only ever likely to be limited traffic potential. One of these was the Basingstoke and Alton route, just over 14 miles

The first design of true LSWR car, No 2 from the H12 class. Livery wise, the H12 type continued the LSWR loco style of having the engine portion in green lined out as per contemporary practice/fashion. This large area of paint was not easy on the eye despite an attempt to reduce the appearance by having the engine number painted centrally. Presumably works/build plates were fitted to all the cars but none of these are apparent from the images. Carriage portions were in standard LSWR colours continued around the end. Edwardian cleaning standards meant patterns were regularly made using tallow and the like on the plain sides.
Ian Wilkins collection

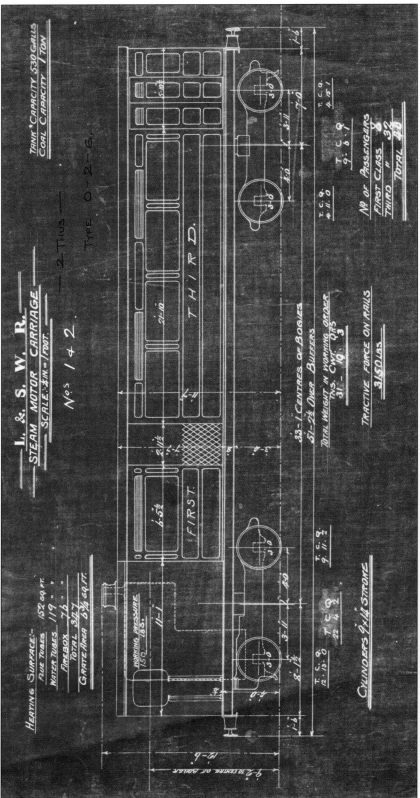

of railway linking the two towns but serving no real purpose other than the politics of preventing an interloper, in this case the GWR, from considering expansion south from their own line at Basingstoke towards the coast. The fact that it was of little strategic importance is proven by the fact that the LSWR took the opportunity to close it in 1917 although its successor, the Southern Railway, were reluctantly compelled to effect a reopening in 1924. It finally closed for good in 1932 (passengers) but was immortalised in the two films 'Oh Mr Porter' (1937) and 'The Wrecker' (1929).[3]

Whatever, the new vehicles were otherwise similar (although certainly not identical) in principal as the dimensions show.

Nos 1 and 2 Order (Class) No H12	As built
Overall length	51' 2½"
Total wheelbase	41' 1"
Bogie wheelbase	8' 0"
Wheel diameter	3' 0"
Cylinders 2 (outside)	9" x 14"
Boiler diameter	3' 1"
Boiler length	2' 2"
Firebox length	3' 10"
Heating surface:	
Tubes	152 sq ft
Firebox	76 sq ft
Cross water tubes	119 sq ft
Working pressure	150 psi
Grate area	6¾ sq ft
Water capacity	530 gallons
Coal capacity	1 ton
Weights in working order	
Engine bogie	22t 4cwt 2qtrs
Trailing bogie	9t 6cwt 1qtr
Total weight	31t 12cwt
Seating capacity	
First class	8
Third class	32

No 1 also taken at Eastleigh when brand new. Great hopes had been expressed in the steam railmotor design with its frugal use of fuel. This view was prior to its use on the Basingstoke & Alton line where it will be noted that no vacuum brake hose is fitted at the end; how then did a locomotive successfully assist the car when required? Certainly a vacuum hose was present a couple of months later when the same car was working from Plymouth. No doubt the need for a tow on occasions had quickly rendered this necessary. *Curl collection*

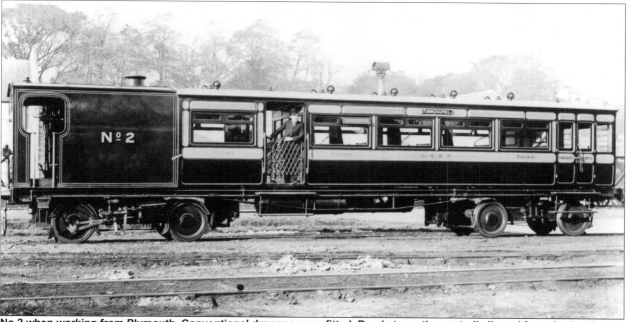

No 2 when working from Plymouth. Conventional drawgear was fitted. Brackets on the cantrail allowed for a destination board to be fitted on the sides and of course a vacuum brake hose is present. Again it is not believed any rail traffic was handled. *Southern Times collection*

Unfortunately, despite the theoretical increase in power available through the additional heating surface and cylinder dimensions, the railcars were a failure on the Basingstoke and Alton line where sharp curves of 12 chains radius, allied to gradients as steep as 1 in 50, meant stalling was a regular occurrence. Under such circumstances assistance had to be summoned from Basingstoke with consequential delays. It is not believed any sanding was provided although this not been fully confirmed.

This failure itself is worthy of comment. Drummond would certainly have been aware of the poor performance of No 1 at Stroud, could he really have expected a similar car to work successfully on another line where the gradients were even steeper, allied now with sharp curves? It must have been obvious to several this would be the likely outcome, perhaps it was the fearsome reputation of Drummond himself that prevented the doubters from speaking out.

The time spend on the Basingstoke and Alton line was therefore brief, just seven weeks from 1 July until 12 August 1904, services thereafter reverting to being loco hauled for the rest of the life of the line. Initial and subsequent employment for the vehicles is as detailed below.

Vehicle No 1	Dates	Work	Notes
	1-7-1904 to 12-8-1904	Basingstoke and Alton line	
	12-8-1904 to ?	Trials on local services, Bournemouth and possibly Plymouth areas	
	1-10-1904	Botley to Bishop's Waltham branch trains	
	May 1906	Aldershot and Alton trials	Trial with 50 fully equipped soldiers to test vehicle suitability in the event of mobilisation
	?	Winchester Cheesehill and Southampton Docks trials	Ditto
	August 1906	Highbridge and Burnham trials	Ventilation in hot weather considered a problem. At peak times incapable of taking all intending passengers
	Autumn / winter 1906	Botley to Bishop's Waltham branch trains	
	Late 1912	Royal Pier – Southampton Town working	
	Late 1912/ early 1913	Transferred to Strawberry Hill – as per No 2 below	
	October 1914		Laid aside

Opposite: No 1 at the Bishop's Waltham terminus of the short branch from Botley. Poor ventilation was a passenger complaint even in the short time the cars were initially working between Basingstoke and Alton and, as seen from the table, also later. So far as the former was concerned, how much of this was down to the time of year, summer, is not reported. *John Bosworth collection*

Vehicle No 2	Dates	Work	
	1-7-1904 to 12-8-1904	Basingstoke and Alton line	
	12-8-1904 to ?	Trials on local services, Plymouth and possibly Bournemouth areas	
	? to February 1910	Local services Plymouth area including the Turnchapel branch	
	February 1910 to February 1915	Transferred to Strawberry Hill for Gunnersbury – Hounslow – Twickenham services, extended to Kingston on Sundays	
	February 1915 to November 1916	Waterloo, Clapham Junction and suburban stations	Parcels and staff transport

The Station Bishops Waltham

Both vehicles were withdrawn in November 1916, recorded mileages were 117,592 and 137,779 respectively, equivalent to 8,710 and 10,206 miles annually; not perhaps a vast amount but respectable considering most journeys would have been of limited distance.

Although numbered 1 and 2 in locomotive listings, they were also given a carriage number, 4201 and 4202. Again, as per the carriage portions of the joint railcars, the carriage sections were subsequently converted for motor-train service in early 1919. Meanwhile the boiler units were evidently still considered to have some useful life and were passed to the War Department at Kimmel Camp in North Wales where they were re-employed on stationary duty.

The LSWR Sectional Appendix to the Rule Book (undated but likely circa 1906) provides a short section and useful information on the 'Working of Rail Motor Trains'. Not all the comments applied to all types but the information was probably included to cover every eventuality both current and likely to occur in the future. Specific local instructions would also have applied to certain routes worked.

"The Cars must be dealt with as ordinary Passenger Trains when running in passenger service and as Light Engines when running empty.

"The cars are constructed to carry 1st and 3rd Class Passengers. No 2nd class accommodation is provided, and 2nd Class tickets must not be issued locally to Passengers who wish to travel by the Cars, but the holders of return halves of 2nd Class tickets and 2nd Class season tickets may be allowed to travel 1st Class in the Cars.

"A compartment to hold about 1 ton of Passengers' luggage is provided in each Car.

"The Cars are fitted with the vacuum automatic and hand brakes which can be operated from either end. A Driver and a Fireman will be

No 1 at the junction station of Botley between October and November 1904. The sheen on the side of the engine compartment may be noted. *Botley & Curdridge Local History Society*

provided on each Car and the Driver must on all occasions ride at the leading end of the vehicle.

"Passengers must not be allowed to smoke in the Car.

"The Car must carry the Head Signals applicable to the Line over which it works.

"If necessary, a coach may be attached to the Car as a Trailer, and provided a coach is not attached, one or two horse boxes, or other such four-wheeled vehicle, may be attached to the rear of the Car, but these vehicles must be fitted with the vacuum automatic brake.

"When an ordinary coach is attached to a Car as a Trailer, the Passengers joining at the halts must, if there is room, ride in the Car in order that tickets may be issued to them.

"The Conductor-Guard must use every care in getting the Passengers into and out of the Car safely and quickly, and must not permit Passengers to ride on the gangway between the 1st and 3rd Class compartments.

"Tickets held by Passengers in the Car must be examined by the Conductor-Guard, and the tickets of Passengers alighting at the Halts must be collected by him.

"Should the Driver at the leading end of the vehicle require the assistance of the brakes worked from the rear end of the Car, he must give three or more short sharp whistles, and the man at the rear must then immediately apply the brakes.

"The Passenger compartments in the Cars are fitted with Pintech's patent system of incandescent gas lighting, and the Conductor-Guard must see that the Cars are lighted as and when required."

The H13 Railmotors, Nos 3 to 15.

The H13 probably had the most pleasing livery of the three types with salmon pink and brown for everything above the solebar and LSWR green on the wheels, cylinders and power bogie. The coach itself was also lined out in gold. The combination worked well. *Ian Wilkins collection*

We come now to the final LSWR railmotor design and certainly also the most numerous. As with the other steam railmotors designs of the LSWR, they too were fitted with outside Walschaerts valve gear driving a single axle.

Drummond had earlier attempted to obtain authority for this build of seven additional units on 5 November 1904, but with the failure of the H12 class on the Basingstoke and Alton line just a few months earlier no doubt ringing in their ears, Board permission was withheld until a report was available of their performance on both the Bishop's Waltham branch and Plymouth area duties. Fortunately this was much more satisfactory and approval for the additional seven vehicles, at an estimated cost of £1,475 each (£188,355 in 2021), was confirmed six months later on 3 May 1905.

The sphere of activity for the new vehicles was anticipated as being:

Whitchurch – Fullerton

Poole – Bournemouth – Christchurch

Wadebridge – Bodmin – Padstow

Plymouth – Turnchapel

As with the H12 vehicles, certain other services would be handed over to the class later and especially as more of the type were built but it is also interesting to note certain lines which might otherwise have been expected to have benefitted from their use appear never to have been considered / worked. Amongst these were Gosport – Stokes Bay, Grateley – Amesbury – Bulford, Petersfield – Midhurst, and even the Meon Valley line. No doubt there were others.

Construction was again Nine Elms / Eastleigh whilst externally the design was such that the whole now presented a neat appearance with coach salmon and brown from the outset. The first seven and the later batch together with their subsequent lifespan, some cars having detail changes (see text), were completed and released to traffic for running in / use as under:

No	Completed	Order No	Carriage No	Withdrawn
3	10/1905	H13	4314	7/1919
4	11/1905	H13	4315	7/1919
5	12/1905	H13	4306	11/1916
6	12/1905	H13	4307	11/1916
7	1/1906	H13	4308	11/1916
8	1/1906	H13	4309	11/1916
9	2/1906	H13	4310	11/1916
10	3/1906	H13	4260	7/1919
11	3/1906	H13	4316	11/1916
12	5/1906	A12	4311	11/1916
13	5/1906	A12	4312	11/1916
14	6/1906	B14	4313	11/1916
15	6/1906	B14	4317	11/1916

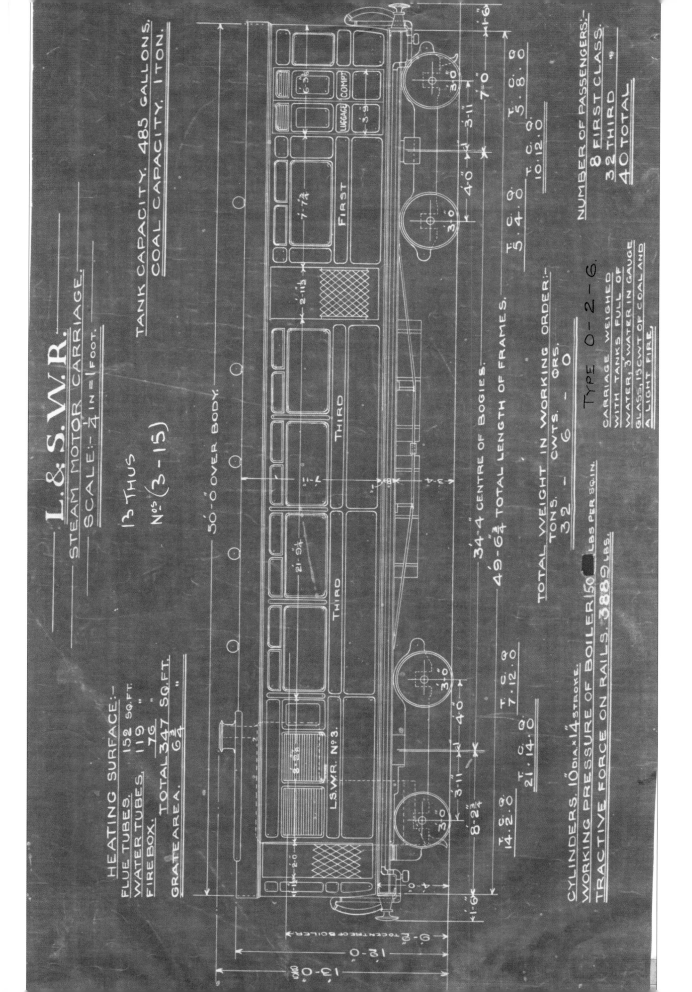

L. & S.W.R.

STEAM MOTOR CARRIAGE.

SCALE :- ¼ IN = 1 FOOT.

Is THUS

Nos (3-15)

HEATING SURFACE :-
FLUE TUBES. 152 SQ.FT.
WATER TUBES. 119 "
FIRE BOX. 76 "
TOTAL 347 SQ.FT.
GRATE AREA. 6¾ "

TANK CAPACITY. 485 GALLONS.
COAL CAPACITY. 1 TON.

NUMBER OF PASSENGERS :-
8 FIRST CLASS.
32 THIRD "
40 TOTAL "

34'-4 CENTRE OF BOGIES.
49'-6¼ TOTAL LENGTH OF FRAMES.
50'-0 OVER BODY.

TOTAL WEIGHT IN WORKING ORDER :-
TONS. CWTS. QRS.
32 - 6 - 0

TYPE 0-2-6.

CARRIAGE WEIGHED
WITH TANKS FULL OF
WATER, 3 WATER IN GAUGE
GLASS, 15 CWT OF COAL AND
A LIGHT FIRE.

CYLINDERS. 10" DIA x 14" STROKE.
WORKING PRESSURE OF BOILER 150 LBS PER SQ. IN.
TRACTIVE FORCE ON RAILS. 3889 LBS.

L.S.W.R. No 3.

The move away from the H13 order is explained by the access changes referred to in the text although it does also seem to infer there were in fact two separate modifications – details of which are not known. Dimensions were as shown in the table.

From Eastleigh it was a simple case of running in each vehicle on the conveniently close Bishop's Waltham line after which the initial disposition was:

Bournemouth: Nos 3 and 4. From here they commenced duty on 5 November 1905 working Poole to Christchurch with extensions to New Milton or Ringwood via Hurn from 1 March 1906.

Nos 5 and 6 were sent to Exmouth Junction and took over Exeter – Whimple – Sidmouth Junction services on 26 January 1906. Later, from 31 May 1908 they worked between Exeter and Topsham; this was after the branch had been doubled and additional halts provided.

No 7 went to Plymouth where it joined H12 No 2 on Friary – Turnchapel services, some of these workings extended to St Budeaux from 26 September 1906.

Guildford had Nos 8 and 9. The first did not remain long before being moved to Plymouth whilst No 9 worked between Bentley and Bordon from 7 March 1906.S

Six further vehicles were ordered in pairs between May and November 1905. Experience with the original seven however had shown that access for servicing could be improved and consequently these six were fitted with two large doors and a removable floor section so that the engine could be separated from the carriage without having to lift the boiler clear of the bogie. What visible alterations may have resulted to the external appearance of the cars is not immediately apparent.

With the six additional units available, allocations and duties would also change, No

Nos 3 to 9 Order (Class) No H13	As built
Overall length	52' 7"
Total wheelbase	42' 2"
Bogie wheelbase	7' 11"
Wheel diameter	3' 0"
Cylinders 2 (outside)	10" x 14"
Boiler diameter	Not given
Boiler length	Not given
Firebox length	Not given
Heating surface:	
Flue tubes	152 sq ft
Firebox	76 sq ft
Water tubes	119 sq ft
Working pressure	150 psi
Grate area	
Water capacity	485 gallons
Coal capacity	1 ton
Weights in working order	32 tons 6cwt
Engine bogie	21T 14cwt
Trailing bogie	10T 12cwt
Total weight	32T 6cwt
Seating capacity	40
First class	8
Third class	32
Tractive effort	3,889 lbs

10 replacing No 8 on Bordon branch duties, Andover having No 11 together with H2 No 2, whilst Wadebridge was allocated Nos 13 and 4. Bournemouth took No 15.

An example of how the new vehicles were received may be given from the Andover units which were originally intended to limit their operation between Whitchurch, Hurstbourne and Fullerton from 1 June 1906. Popularity however was such that in the up direction one journey was extended to Basingstoke with the corresponding down working running direct from Basingstoke to Andover Junction, where Bradley comments, '…a reversal was necessary to reach the (Andover) Town station'. By implication this means the services were actually; Andover Junction – Andover Town, thence south to Fullerton – reverse – Hurstbourne and Whitchurch. As was also the case in the London area involving joint car No 2, from Andover at night the spare unit was used for staff journeys; conveying relief signalmen, permanent way men as well as coal and water supplied to outlying locations. This might sound slightly strange in the 21st century but it must be remembered that many of these intermediate locations were indeed isolated and deliveries by rail were relied upon.

On the same date that the Whitchurch – Fullerton service commenced, 1 June 1906, so in the west Nos 13 and 4 commenced duty west from Wadebridge to Padstow and east from Wadebridge to Bodmin. No 15 also ran trials from Bere Alston to Callington. Unfortunately the contours of this route, allied to the fact that sanding was not fitted, defeated the attempt.

Bradley also recounts an amusing episode from contemporary history when in October 1906 the vicar at Bodmin unsuccessfully approached the LSWR to have car No 13 renumbered. He did not succeed.

Interior heating appears not to have been provided and there were no toilets. Passengers might thus prefer a conventional train but railmotor services were often afforded a cheaper ticket as running costs were cheaper and this was passed on to the public to encourage patronage. The lack of amenities would not have been an issue with the joint cars on the Southsea branch where the same basic passenger facilities were common between the railway and the street trams – there were no toilets and no heating whether this be by horse drawn or electric traction tram. In addition journeys to Southsea or Fratton were short. Not always the case on some of the other routes worked. Might even the popularity of the vehicles in the Andover area have been due as much to novelty value? Car No 10 is seen here at Bishop's Waltham with the seemingly superfluous corridor connection. Left to right are long serving branch Guard George Padwick, Postman Edgar Adams, Porter Signalman Steve Goulding, Fireman Frank Willis, and Driver Perkins. *John Bosworth collection*

Even before the poor experience of No 15 running on the PDSW line from Bere Alston, Drummond had designed a further three vehicles intended to work between Plymouth and Tavistock. These would have cost £2,080 each and would have been enlarged to provide 40% more power, be fitted with steam sanding, variable blast pipes, feedwater heating and electric light. The order was recorded for 7 March 1906. The additional power available would also have enabled a new design of trailing car having 32 third-class seats to be hauled whilst at the end of this trailer would be fitted driving controls. Through communication between vehicles would have been by a conventional gangway. We are not told if the pair would run as a 'permanently coupled set' or if the rail motor unit would also have been capable of being driven from either end if running solo but likely this would have been the case considering the comments by the Board of Trade from around this time. Similarly no information is given on whether the duplicate driving controls would have been activated by mechanical, compressed air or some other means of control. These vehicles would have been numbered outside the series as Nos 26-28. Possibly but as it turns out, fortuitously, Nine Elms had not progressed the order to any extend by the end of March, which

Opposite top: Car No 3 at an unreported location. Was the member of the crew intent on being in the photograph – photography still being a bit of a novelty – or might it have been to escape the heat of the cab, although it may be noted the front window appears to be closed. *Commercial postcard*

Opposite bottom: Another unreported location with the vehicle being driven from the trailing end. The headcode indicates a possible Ringwood service. Unlike the GWR steam railmotors, passenger steps for low platform or intermediate ground level access were not provided on any of the LSWR designs. The LSWR did build some new halts on parts of their system commensurate with railmotor use but the majority of these appear to have had conventional height platforms. *Commercial postcard*

Above: Rural Hampshire. An unidentified car at Calcot bridge between Botley and Bishop's Waltham, circa 1909. The seating type, wood or upholstery, for third class passengers in the H12 and H13 type series is not known. *Jack Tickner*

is itself unusual as previous work had been completed rapidly. Whatever, folklore has it that Drummond was informed the GWR had progressed to the use of a '517' class 0-4-2T with three trailers (likely sandwiched in a 2+1 arrangement), consequently work was quickly halted on the new vehicles and an alternative design prepared for a small locomotive which could perform a similar task. This would take the form of the C14, although the development of this design is outside the remit of the present work.

As seen from the earlier Bishop's Waltham image, for reasons that do not appear logical, a corridor connection did appear at the opposite end to the boiler on vehicles 10 and 11, perhaps more in hope than actuality as they would surely have been incapable of taking a passenger trailer.

Despite the promise the steam railmotor concept showed, it was the ingress of dirt, soot and ashes inherent with a steam environment that was the major disadvantage of the concept. Simply put, passenger carriages were understandably not stored or serviced in a steam shed for obvious reasons and this dirt became a major problem to the railcars. Consequently it became practice to stable the railcars away from the actual shed wherever possible whilst surfaces were wiped down and cleaned on a regular basis. With labour both cheap and plentiful it was not a management issue, although at a lower level it became a staff irritant.

Bradley gives us some useful coal consumption and running costs comparisons on certain of the services operated by the steam railmotors including a working from Guildford not previously mentioned:

	Coal Consumption (lbs) per train mile		
	Railcar (class not specified)	Motor tank (class not specified but presumably a later comparison with a C14)	Class O2
Guildford – Farnham	16.3	20.1	30.6
Botley – Bishop's Waltham	11.1	16.9	28.9
Bournemouth – New Milton	12.1	21.2	29.7
Gunnersbury – Twickenham	17.3	-	31.8
Plymouth Friary – St Budeaux / Turnchapel	11.2	19.2	31.4
Bentley - Bordon	13.2	18.6	26.8
Average	13.5	19.2	29.9

Taking the same routes, we are also given the equivalent running costs per mile

	d.		
Guildford – Farnham	3.7	6.3	10.6
Botley – Bishop's Waltham	3.1	5.8	9.4
Bournemouth – New Milton	3.4	5.6	11.5
Gunnersbury – Twickenham	3.9	-	10.8
Plymouth Friary – St Budeaux / Turnchapel	3.9	6.1	10.3
Bentley - Bordon	3.4	5.7	11.1
Average	3.6	5.9	10.6

Based on the above, there are clear advantages to the railmotor and confirmation of the earlier comment that it is surprising the concept was not developed further, on the basis of the costs savings alone. Variations relevant to each line are explained by factors such as gradients, the number of stops and also loads.

Having turned back to what were in effect locomotive hauled trains in certain areas, a rearrangement of allocations and duties meant that by 1 January 1907 the services were as follows:

Guildford: Nos 7, 9 and 10. Duties still included Bentley to Bordon but now also Guildford to Farnham via Aldershot (reverse). No 4 also moved to Fratton, where it was tried on services across the top of the Farlington triangle so forming a shuttle between Havant and Cosham for passengers on through journeys. Already such travellers were forced to detrain and then entrain twice in a short distance; this was not helped by the limited luggage space provided in the railcars. Circumstances when a trailing car, perhaps devoted to luggage, would have been useful but an even easier solution was the return to a locomotive hauled service as was indeed the case. Whilst at Fratton whether No 4 also did service on the Southsea branch is not reported.

A new venture for the LSWR cars was on another joint line, that to Portland. As partner with the LSWR, it was the GWR who had agreed to build two railcars for the service. For reasons that are not reported these did not appear and upon the opening of the new station at Melcombe Regis in 1909 services were instead worked by an LSWR vehicle, No 12, although No 4, by now moved from Fratton (and possibly elsewhere), was present at Christmas the same year. Once more as with earlier experience at Southsea, peak time overcrowding was a difficulty and a C14 and trailers took over just a few days later on 1 January 1910.

A Bodmin service although the location is not confirmed. The vehicle is not positively identified but could be No 8. On both the H12 and H13 (plus variants) designs, driving controls were provided at both ends from the outset. Exactly what these were are not reported but likely to have been limited to a regulator, brake and whistle. No 12 at least had received a modification to the boiler end windows by around 1908. Now instead of three windows across the front with the centre one only capable of being opened, it was superseded by small vertical windows on the extremities and a pair of centre opening windows. Heat in the cab likely prompted the change. Note also the 'gate' rather than a conventional door to the sides of the driving compartment. *Southern Times collection*

Back in Hampshire the short branch from Fort Brockhurst to Lee-on-the-Solent was being operated by the LSWR and was then formally taken over in August 1909. No 9 was the first user although a month later, on 1 September, No 10 became the regular unit, although without costings for this working available it is difficult to see if even steam railmotor use could prevent a haemorrhaging of costs equivalent to a loss of slightly over £408 in 1908. It is not mentioned where the car may have been stabled overnight and the assumption is this was at Gosport. Somehow this branch managed to survive with passenger services operating until 1930 and goods for five years after that.

As the advantage of flexibility in working applicable to the use of a separate motor tank and trailer coaches became ever more apparent, the steam railmotors were slowly superseded on their existing duties and whilst some depots lost their allocations completely, others were permitted to retain spare cars to cover failures in traffic. Exactly what reliability had been beforehand is not reported as spare capacity is not previously mentioned.

Concurrent with this, certain services in the London area were similarly given over to railmotor working and from information available appear to have been principally off peak services. In addition there was a return to more familiar routes.

Thus from 1 January 1910 Gunnersbury – Hounslow – Twickenham trains (extended to Kingston on Sundays) were operated by Nos 2, 4 and 8. (Bradley again provides these details but does he mean LSWR No 2 or is he in fact referring to joint car No 2 which as mentioned was in operation here from the following month?) Slightly before this from 9 December 1909, No 1 and No 11 were tasked with Southampton Town to the Royal Pier workings, this in itself very much a street tramway operation. Occasional visits being made to Southampton West and as far north as Winchester (LSWR or GWR not specified). Once more, was this K11 or H12 No 1 that is being referred to?

Aesthetically there was also a slight change to the identifications with loco numbers moved from the buffer beam to above the end windows. This probably commenced with No 6 in May 1913. More interesting perhaps was the addition of a small letter after each number; 'P' for the trailing end and 'D' at the engine end. Why this should have been is not certain but the thought has to be this was to assist station staff in identifying the position of the luggage compartment as the unit arrived at a station. Both the H12 and H13 (and variants of the latter) had their luggage compartments at the non engine end but it would not have assisted with the joint cars where the opposite applied. Practically too loading luggage, and the time taken to achieve this, would have been of little consequence on a quiet branch line with relaxed timings applied, but perhaps it was a different matter on a heavily trafficked route. (Decades later the 'Hampshire DEMUS' were similarly designated with an inverted black triangle on the yellow panel/ end and for the same purpose.)

Further development of the motor train principal in the middle of 1912 saw an 'M7' and the former LBSCR 'Terrier' now LSWR No 735 equipped for motor train operation – an obvious development of the railmotor and C14 principals. With success achieved in this form, services left to the railmotors declined further. By July 1914 only the Bishop's Waltham, Royal Pier, Wadebridge area, and Gunnersbury services were still operating. These involved units most recently repaired, Nos 3, 4, 7, 9, 10, 11 and 13.

One month later came the advent of WW1 and consequently there was no wish to attempt to attract additional passenger traffic. Accordingly the Royal Pier service ceased along with the Gunnersbury services – the former at least would never resume. This left the sole railcar services as those from Wadebridge from where Nos 3, 4 and 10 were active.

Aside from previous comments relative to the use of the joint car No 2 at this time, the others were laid aside with apparently no work. This continued until November 1916 when Nos 5, 6,

No 10 at Bodmin. Why Drummond persisted with drive to a single axle is not known but this would also be the case on the original C14 design and remember of course his famed 'double singles' comprising the solitary 'T7' and five examples of the 'E10' classes. *Southern Times collection*

7,8 ,9, 11, 12, 13, 14 and 15 were condemned. Nos 11, 14 and 15 having their carriage portions converted to trailers fairly quickly. Following withdrawal the remaining units were stored at Micheldever, possibly for as much as three years. Bradley is not totally clear on the fate of the other coach units from the batch withdrawn at this time, but it appears likely they too were converted but in this case not until 1919.

Official records for these also show that subsequent to withdrawal / conversions, the major remaining components, viz the engine and boiler units, were not finally broken up until January although prior to this most of the boilers had been sold off to market gardeners as greenhouse heating.

This left Nos 2, 4 and 10 (the Bodmin Vicar did not now have to see No 13 anymore), all three of which received general repairs between March and June 1916 and returned to the westerly outpost of Wadebridge, at first continuing to work to both Padstow and Bodmin but latterly to Bodmin only. This continued until March 1918 when this working too was replaced by a motor train. Officially they were still on the stock book until July of the same year but it is doubtful they did any revenue earning service between March and July. Final mileages for the three were 188,462, 196,329, and 192,996. As before the carriage portions were once again converted.

Summarising the railmotor story on the LSWR is not easy. With hindsight it is all too easy to be subjective. Objectively it must be said the LSWR and the other companies that developed similar vehicles were learning as they went along. Could the LSWR cars have been better – certainly – but we should not forget they worked for some years over a number of lines. A more powerful power unit was really what was required plus the ability to haul a trailer, both of course nearly coming to fruition. As it was, nearly all the companies that tried similar vehicles would eventually phase them out in favour of a locomotive hauled train but it was not an overnight change. The steam railmotor concept was simply a step in the development of railway passenger travel, one might even say a step in the direction of the multiple unit trains we have today.

Opposite top: Bournemouth Central whilst working between Poole and possibly Ringwood. This is No 3. *Commercial postcard*

Opposite bottom: In the same area; passing through Talbot woods on the way to Bournemouth West. *Commercial postcard Pouteau series / Stephenson Locomotive Society collection*

Above: The home of so many of the cars; the branch to Bishop's Waltham and the junction with the Eastleigh to Fareham line at Botley; the branch may be seen curving away in the right distance. The working timetable would indicate which services were worked by the steam railmotors, a capital 'M' or the word 'Motor' being displayed at the top of the relevant column. Details of failures or difficulties in service are not reported, except that is for one occasion around 18 February 1906 when No 5 burst a cylinder on the first run of the day on the Bishop's Waltham line. Botley station and the surrounding area would deal with copious quantities of strawberries and other soft fruit in the summer season. *Commercial postcard*

(1)   The administration of the East Southsea branch was a strange affair which had its roots in the agreement that existed between the two companies for pooling resources at Portsmouth. So far as the branch was concerned, this meant each concern would provide staff for the line on an alternate annual basis, meaning on 31 December each year one company's men would pick up their belongings and depart to be replaced the next morning by those of the other concern. See *The Southsea Railway*. Published by Kingfisher Railway Productions, 1985.

(2)   Mr T. Hurry Richards, in conjunction with Mr Sidney B. Haslam, jointly produced a paper on railmotors for the proceedings of the Institute of Mechanical Engineers, Vol 71, p651-718, 1 June 1906.

(3)   See 'The Basingstoke and Alton Light Railway', Barton Publishing, 2003.

References:

Aside from those books previously mentioned in the text, the following published work and sources have been consulted:

'The Bishop's Waltham Branch', Wild Swan Publications, 1988.

National Archives MT6/1402/2. The writer is also grateful to Gerry Nichols for access to the SLS archive, Roger Simmonds and Ian Wilkins.

Next time the G6 0-6-0T. Future instalments will include detail on the railcar / railmotors of the SECR and LBSCR.

The Southern from the Air
(Unless stated images are from the family archive of the late Alan Elliott)

To some, the title of this pictorial piece may well be taken to mean images of Waterloo, Clapham Junction and the like – not this time. Instead we have taken as our theme a more 'rural' approach with just six images depicted in alphabetical order.

We start with Betteshanger colliery in Kent. Named after the nearby village and close to Deal in East Kent, this was the largest of the collieries in the Kent coalfield and operated from 1927 until 1989. Other collieries in Kent were Chislet, Snowsdown and Tilmanstone but Betteshanger was the largest.

Betteshanger. Coal was first found in the Lydden valley near Deal in December 1912 at a depth of just under 1,500ft. How this came about is not reported and in the meanwhile no progress was made. After WW1 however, the firm of Dorman Long (in later years better known for their steel products) purchased the mineral rights to large areas of land in the Deal area. When burnt, Kent coal fired at a high temperature thus making it suitable for the steel industry and it was for this reason that Dorman Long desired their own supply.

Soon after making this purchase, Dorman Long & Co. joined forces with another company, Messrs. S. Pearson & Sons (who had built the Admiralty Harbour at Dover), to form Pearson & Dorman Long Ltd. This company had a controlling interest in the Channel Steel Company which had also proved the existence of 100 million tons of iron ore near Dover. Might this have also been the S. Pearson who had been involved in railway construction in the latter part of the 19th and early years of the twentieth century? If so the family seat was at Cowdray Park, Midhurst.

The joint concern constructed a railway just over two miles long on the west side of the line north of Deal on the Kent coast to the site of the Betteshanger colliery. Here the first shaft was sunk on 19 May 1924. Plans at the time were for further mines at Wingham, Fleet, Woodnesborough, Stodmarsh and Deal.

As the largest mine in the area, Betteshanger had shafts 24ft in diameter. During sinking the shafts flooded twice, but by sealing the sides with cement (using the cementation process) progress continued and the coal seam was reached three years later.

With coal now accessible, some 1,500 miners and their families descended literally overnight on the area. Where these came from it is not reported but it can only have been from mines elsewhere in the country, lured perhaps by promises of a better standard of income and a coastal lifestyle. At the time Deal might well have been described as a genteel seaside resort and the arrival of such numbers of workers was not universally welcomed. Contemporary newspaper reports refer to '…rough and dirty men with unintelligible accents'. Lodging houses, cafes and pubs soon had signs up saying 'no miners' while butchers and grocers sold the worst quality goods as cheap miner's specials. Exactly where such an influx might have been accommodated at first is not reported as it was not until 1929 that the farmlands of Mill Hill on the outskirts of Deal were acquired for a new colliery estate. Meanwhile some deputies' (foreman's) houses had been provided near the pit. Pithead baths were not available until 1934.

Over the years Betteshanger acquired a reputation as being worked by a number of men with particularly hard line attitudes. This was accentuated when some union men arrived following the General Strike of 1926 who had been blacklisted at their previous pits.

As examples of militant behaviour, in 1938 a strike was called when some of the pit boys refused to accept the behaviour of the two deputies responsible for their supervision. Later the same day, the rest of the pit boys and all the colliers joined the walk out, largely due to the fact that the pit could not run properly without the pit boys. Work was only resumed after agreement was given to hold a public enquiry.

Betteshanger was also the only pit to strike during the Second World War. The colliers' reason for striking was over allowances for working a difficult seam and because these conditions changed from week to week. This resulted in three union officials being imprisoned and over 1,000 men being given the option of a fine or hard labour. The authorities were keen to suppress the strike as there was a danger it could spread to other mines whilst the Government could not afford such a strike in the middle of a war. All but nine of the miners refused to pay. In the face of having to find prison spaces for 1,000 men, the Government decided to take no action and released the three imprisoned officials.

Despite being a profitable pit with plenty of reserves of good quality coal, Betteshanger was never really allowed to develop to its full potential and under the nationalised coal board was allocated restricted quotas whilst the available market also held back production.

Probably the final trade dispute was the miners' strike of 1984-5, Betteshanger being the last colliery in the country to return to work. It would only be for a short time as it would close in 1989, coincidentally also the final coal mine at work in Kent.

In the illustration the deputies' houses may be seen on the inside of a circular road; this circuit was apparently used by miners to race their whippets.

Something over 250 miles west of Deal and 750' above sea level is Okehampton. No coal mines here but instead we are in the land of granite with Meldon Quarry, not visible in the image, sited south of the station. In this view we are looking from the south towards Sampford Courtenay and eventually Coleford Junction (for Exeter) and with access to and from the town – the latter at a lower level to the railway – via the roadway at left bottom. As an operational station for passengers, the station had a working life of 101 years from 1871 to 1972. Through trains between Exeter and Plymouth had ceased to operate from 1968 and from this time until 1972 it was served by a shuttle service to and from Exeter. How such a passenger service had managed to survive supporting a local community of just 4,000 is open to question, but likely due to the presence of the quarry at Meldon. Perhaps BR in their naivety considered that at Okehampton, as well as elsewhere, railway passengers whose local station had been closed would simply jump into their cars to avail themselves of the nearest rail facility. It did not happen, for once sat in the seat of the family car this became the preferred method of travel for work or leisure. The line through Okehampton continued to survive due to the existence of the quarry, that is until costings revealed transporting limestone, used as ballast by the railway network, could be brought even more cheaply by ship from Scotland to Tilbury than by rail from Devon. Consequently, the quarry ceased production in 2011.

Fortunately the station building had survived and found a new use as a skills centre with an independent model shop and café also on site. The former goods shed was also converted into a youth hostel. A railway heritage centre was established whilst a private company operated trains between Meldon through Okehampton to Sampford Courtenay. In addition a summer service operated from the public network at Exeter forming part of the Dartmoor Sunday Rover network. Occasional visits were also made by enthusiast special trains including at least one with a '2 +10' HST set which passed through Okehampton to reach Meldon. Heritage line services ceased from 24 December 2019.

Then in November 2017 the Government announced the reopening of the line to Okehampton from Coleford Junction to be part of the national network and services commenced on 20 November 2021. Whilst any hope for a full restoration of services over the 'Withered Arm' to places such as Bude, Padstow and Ilfracombe is little more than a pipe dream, the hoped for revival of the route south of Okehampton through Tavistock to link into the network again at Bere Alston is a possibility many would welcome as well as providing a useful diversion should Dawlish become impassable again in the future consequence of storm conditions.

In the photograph, undated but taken post June 1972 as the signalling has been removed, the locomotive facilities previously north of the station on the west side of the line have already been demolished and the main running line reduced to a single track.

Back to the south east now and to Rye on the line between Hastings and Ashford. Opened in 1864 the main building was in Italianate stye designed by William Tress. (Tress was also responsible for the station at Battle – both are now, rightly, listed buildings.)

In typical South Eastern fashion, the platforms are staggered and are seen here linked with an 'Exmouth Junction' style open concrete footbridge. This had been provided in the early 1960s as the route was originally included in the Phase 2 of the Kent Coast electrification scheme. In the event electrification plans were abandoned and the line remains diesel worked to this day.

In the photograph an extension may be seen to the right of the original building. This was a parcels office provided by the Southern Railway, fortunately built in sympathy to the main building and replacing a lean-to structure. On the left of the image is Ferry Road level crossing, at this stage still with gates but later replaced by the ubiquitous lifting barriers and CCTV. Goods ceased to be handled in 1963 and the commodious goods shed was demolished just over 20 years later.

From the air we see goods are still being handled and mechanical signalling is present. The latter was controlled from the signal box on the opposite side of the line to the station. This structure too, dating from 1894, was listed in 2013. For decades there was double track through the station and on either side, but rationalisation now means Rye is a simple passing loop with consequential delays to services in both directions should a timetabled crossing move be delayed.

The terminus at Seaford being a branch of the line to Newhaven and which itself is accessed from Lewes. Opened in 1864, Seaford had been intended as an intermediate stopping place on a proposed coastal route to Eastbourne. In the event the section between Seaford and Eastbourne was never built.

From the photograph we can gauge some idea of the facilities as once existed with a main platform and bay, the main platform originally having a traverser at one end rather than an engine release crossover. The traverser afforded access to the run-round loop. There was also an end loading dock plus the usual goods shed and goods yard facilities.

The main station building survives today and although originating from different companies, externally displays a distinct similarity to Netley on the LSWR line between Fareham and St Denys. The building also stands parallel with the platform rather than across the ned so confirming by its position the forlorn hopes for onward expansion.

Despite the lack of goods traffic visible in the photograph, coal staiths are still apparent, indeed local merchants may well have continued to use the now rail-less yard for some time despite now receiving bulk supplies by road.

Another feature apparent from the photograph is the telegraph pole on the road side of the bay platform, another feature associated with railways now long consigned to history.

The line to Seaford was electrified from 7 July 1935 and the last steam train pulled out of the station, it is believed, on 25 July 1963; Terrier No 32678 attached to two vans.

Moving away from the immediate railway environment, the lack of vehicular traffic is another feature, images can so often be dated from the designs of the motor cars in view and here a best guess would be the early 1960s.

Today Seaford remains open as a single track railway with just the one, main platform in use. Ironically this is identified as Platform 2, the former bay long out of use still being counted in the pairing.

Stonegate is one of those locations that rarely seems to receive any mention in railway books. The location here has had three names; the first of these at the time of opening, 1 September 1851, as Witherenden, co-terminus with a nearby hamlet. A change took place just three months later to Ticehurst Road which is how it remained until in the last months of the Southern Railway it was renamed as present from 16 June 1947. (The Ticehurst Road designation is explained as this was the nearest railhead to the town of that name. 'Road' being a fairly common name extension without giving intending passengers any particular clue as to how far they might then have to walk.)

The view is looking south towards Hastings again with the typical South Eastern staggered platform layout. The goods shed was on the same, down side as the main buildings and it will be noted there is also an up refuge siding opposite the main platform.

Serving very much a rural community there was a surprising amount of milk despatched – we tend to associate milk more with the West Country but Sussex and Kent should not be discounted. Unfortunately this traffic was all lost to road by the mid-1930s. Other goods sent were hops, apples and, to an extent, grain of varying types. Incoming was coal for the local merchant and agricultural machinery.

The ornate station building associated with Tunbridge Wells West is out of shot in this aerial view of the west end of the site. Instead we have the locomotive facilities and part of the goods yard complete with its large goods shed. Originally engine facilities had been at a two-road shed and turntable at the opposite end of the site. Top right is a timber yard, once served by its own private siding, coal is again apparent and indeed appears to be the dominant non-passenger traffic. Although undated, identification of the engine bottom right shows this to be a BR Standard Class 4 and so we may therefore date the view as 1950s at least. Outside the shed we also have an SR mogul and what is almost certainly a C2x; identified by the double domes. On the opposite side of the running lines, another 0-6-0 tender engine is engaged in a spot of shunting. Tunbridge Wells West locomotive shed was bombed in November 1940 and the roof here is the replacement. The station suffered by mainly serving cross country rather than main routes yet despite this as a location it remained extremely busy with the timetable showing 70 passenger and five goods workings daily in 1956. Unfortunately the Beeching report and commensurate closure of the routes it had served, East Grinstead to Lewes (the 'Bluebell line'), Eridge to Polegate (the 'Cuckoo line'), Three Bridges to Groombridge, and finally that from Lewes north to Uckfield, meant a continual drop off in traffic allied to which was little if any investment over the years save for basic maintenance.

An indication of this run down may be gauged with facts such as there being 25 steam engines allocated to the depot in 1956, but by 1963 there were none.

The signal box opposite the shed throat was originally 'Tunbridge Wells West' but later simplified to 'Tunbridge Wells A'. 'East' or 'B' box was at the opposite end of the station near the tunnel which formed a spur leading to the Hastings line and so connecting with the Central station in the town.

Part of the site has since been redeveloped but more appropriate is that Tunbridge Wells West now forms the headquarters of the Spa Valley Railway who operate over five miles of line through Groombridge to Eridge where there are interchange facilities with the national network.

- *and speaking of coal…*

In connection with the Betteshanger colliery image, we are pleased to include three other Kent colliery related images. No details unfortunately as to which colliery is depicted first (this page) but information would certainly be welcome.

Opposite top and centre: First we have two views of Chislet Halt, deserted and then with the colliery shift awaiting their train home. This stopping place had opened in 1919 with similar to the basic facilities seen; at a later date Southern Railway style concrete platforms were provided. The colliery of the same name that it served – seen in the background - closed in 1969 although the stopping place was still in use for a further two years. In BR days we see a train approaching behind an LMS design 2-6-4T.

Opposite bottom: Finally a view of a Margate to Chislet colliery special behind 'H' No 1016. The first vehicle, a van, owes its origins to the LBSCR whilst the remaining stock is to LCDR design. Note the sixth passenger vehicle, identified by the additional roof ventilators, is First Class for the use of ordinary passengers. Would it have had any custom? *All images Rev A. Mace / Transport Treasury*

Accident at Eastbourne
Buffer stop collision
23 May 1930

From the Board of Trade enquiry and report of Col A. C. Trench.

"I have the honour to report for the information of the Minister of Transport, in accordance with the Order of the 23 May 1930, the result of my Inquiry into the circumstances of the accident which occurred at 6.53 pm on the 21 May 1930, at Eastbourne (terminus) Station on the Southern Railway.

The 5.20pm express passenger train, Victoria to Eastbourne, collided with the fixed buffer stops of No 3 platform road. A total of 58 passengers and three railway personnel suffered from injuries or shock, but none of the latter had to leave duty. The majority of the injuries were fortunately of a minor nature, only four persons having to be detained in hospital, and the comparatively large number of injured was probably due to the fact that passengers were preparing to alight.

As a result of the collision the leading buffer beam and the main frames of the engine were bent; together with other minor damage.

The headstocks of the leading coach were bent, buffer castings damaged and the body shifted on the underframe, in addition to minor damage to various portions of body and underframe. The underframe of the second coach was buckled at the leading end and very badly buckled at the trailing end, the trailing end compartment being crushed in by the vestibule of the Pullman immediately in rear. The body was driven forward about 25 inches on the underframe and a number of other portions of the body, underframe and bogies were damaged. Pullman No 30, the third coach, had both headstocks bent and a good deal of minor damage throughout; both vestibules were damaged but neither of them collapsed or were crushed. Pullman car Sappho, the fourth coach, together with the sixth and seventh coaches, sustained minor damage in several places, particularly buffer castings. The fifth coach was undamaged.

The buffer beam of the stop and the concrete wall supporting it were broken and the concrete shattered.

The train consisted of seven coaches, apart from two for Seaford which had been detached from the rear at Lewes, marshalled as follows from front to rear :--

Third brake	No 3683	24 tons	Built 1899
First brake	No 7617	23 tons	Built 1905
3rd class Pullman	No 30	32 tons	Built 1922
1st class Pullman	'Sappho'	40 tons	Built 1924
Composite	No 6011	22 tons	Built 1900
Composite	No 6003	22 tons	Built 1901
Third brake	No 3860	24 tons	Build 1900

It was drawn by engine No E.767 Sir Valence, King Arthur Class, type 4-6-0, with 6-wheeled tender, weighing 123 tons in working order.

The overall length of the train and engine was 455 feet and the total weight 310 tons.

The engine was fitted with the vacuum brake on coupled and tender wheels, the percentage of brake power being 49.9. This class of engine is fitted with a crosshead driven vacuum pump in addition to the Dreadnought pattern ejector; the coaches were fitted with the vacuum brake on all wheels.

All coaches were fitted with electric light. The weather was fine and the rail was dry.

Description.

Approaching Eastbourne the line is in a direction generally southerly, with right-hand curvature varying between 60 and 22 chains radius, up to a point some 40 yards inside the outer end of the platform, where the line becomes straight for the last 200 yards to the buffer stops. From the driver's position on a

'King Arthur' class 4-6-0 No 767 Sir Valence. Even at the collision speed of approximately 4mph the impact was, according to the report, sufficient to damage the front buffer beam and main frames. Such damage would be expected to have warranted a works visit, yet the 'Book of ....' * shows no repairs around this time. Two possible conclusions are possible; either the repairs were not reported on the engine record card or they turned out to be less serious than first anticipated and were instead resolved at Stewarts Lane where the engine was then based. No 767 was new in 1925 and remained in service until mid-1959. *Transport Treasury*

King Arthur class engine (left-hand drive) it was found that the buffer stops came into view at a distance of about 210 yards.

The length of the platform is 714 feet from ramp to buffer stops. Distances from Eastbourne No 3 platform buffer stops :—

Eastbourne distant signal 1,380 yards

Outer home signal 576 yards

Inner home and platform distant signals 343 yards

Signal box 300 yards

End of platform ramp 240 yards

The gradient approaching is level for 1½ miles; the immediate entrance to the station consists of about 650 yards rising at 1 in 521, and thereafter 110 yards to the buffer stops rising at 1 in 267.

Report.

The train in question has a booked timing of 93 minutes for the 66 miles Victoria to Eastbourne including stops at Lewes and Polegate, and on the day of the accident it ran in accordance with schedule timings except for one minute lost by a service slack at Balham which was regained before Three Bridges. It left Polegate at booked time, 6.46, and the scheduled speed thence to Eastbourne is 36mph, arriving at Eastbourne at 6.53. It is not the fastest timing of the day between London and Eastbourne and there was no question of running fast to make up time.

In the course of the journey there was a service slack at Barham to 15mph and there are permanent speed restrictions at Keymer Junction and Lewes and Polegate; at both of the latter stations the train is booked to stop.

With the exception of the slack at Keymer Junction which is referred to below, Driver

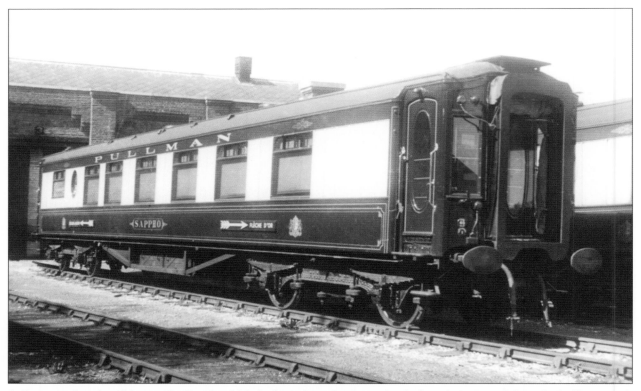

Pullman car Sappho. This was the fourth vehicle in the train and only received minor damage, mainly to the buffing gear. It is seen here some years later at the Pullman works at Preston Park in 'Golden Arrow' livery. *Antony Ford collection*

Suckling had no difficulty in the normal operation of the brakes of his train at any point and stopped at the stations exactly where he intended 'within a yard'.

Approaching Eastbourne, Suckling shut off steam just before reaching the outer distant signal and estimated he was travelling about 35-40mph at this point. He applied the brake as he was approaching the outer home signal, reducing speed to something under 30mph, and he made a further application between the outer and inner home signals (576 and 343 yards from buffer stops). Both these brake applications produced the normal retardation he intended and he had no suspicion that there was anything wrong with the brake.

Before reaching the inner home signal, however, he thought he was pulling up too, quickly and therefore as he passed it he replaced the brake handle in the running position. He estimated that he passed the signal box at 10 to 15mph which he considered normal speed at this point. As he entered the platform he made a further application in order

to stop in the usual place, but he stated that the brake did not seem to take effect although he reduced the vacuum by about 8 to 10 inches.

As soon as he realised that the train was not pulling up as he intended, he made a full application when the brake did take effect. He still thought he would stop clear of the buffer stops and it was not until he was close to them that he realised he could not stop. He then tried to reverse but it was too late, and the engine struck the buffer stops at a speed of about 4mph.

There is a general consensus of evidence that up to the time the engine passed the end of the platform the speed was normal, and it was only when the engine was more than half way down the platform that any of the witnesses thought the speed was higher than normal.

Fireman Atkins had shut off the injector just before entering the platform and applied the hand brake at this point. As far as he could recollect the boiler pressure at this moment was about 160-170lbs., the working pressure being 200lbs. He did not realise that the speed was in any way abnormal or that they were likely to hit the buffer stops until they were a few yards away.

Guard G. E. Garwood tested the brake before leaving Victoria and noted that 21 inches of vacuum was obtained. At Lewes, after detaching the two rear coaches for Seaford, he tested again with the same result. He had noticed nothing abnormal about the working of the brake or the train on the journey and up till the moment when his van was approaching the signal box, by which time the engine would be about entering the platform. He looked out at this point and thought the driver was going a little fast. He then looked at his vacuum gauge and practically at once saw the vacuum destroyed, evidently by a full application of the brake. He applied his hand brake as hard as he could but did not think that as his van entered the platform the train was losing speed as he would have expected with a full brake application. He did not look at the gauge again before the collision.

Driver Suckling, in conversation with an Inspector a few minutes after the accident, said he did not know what had happened. He said that when he was halfway along the platform he thought he could stop, but as he went on towards the buffer stops he made a full brake application, but it seemed to have no effect.

After the accident the brakes were found to be fully applied throughout the train. No sand was used, the rail being dry and in good condition, and there were no signs of any of the wheels having picked up.

On the following day, after a preliminary inquiry, Driver Suckling was discussing the matter with his fireman when he recollected that during the run down, when approaching Keymer Junction, he had made what he considered a normal application of the brake, which he estimated at about 8 ins., but found that the train speed did not seem to fall as quickly as he wanted and he had therefore to make a further application, about 15 ins. on the gauge, before the brake took hold properly. He thought no more of this at the time and when entering Lewes he made a normal application

which he saw by the gauge was 10 ins. with normal and quite satisfactory results. At Polegate also the brake worked normally.

He recollected this incident at Keymer Junction subsequently and, when asked, Fireman Atkins thought he also recollected it. It seemed possible therefore that there might have been some intermittent defect in the operation of the brake. After the accident all brake gear of the engine and coaches was thoroughly examined and found to be in satisfactory condition and working normally, but a small piece of cotton waste was found on the wire cage in the vacuum connecting pipe in the rear of the tender, and this suggested the possibility of some cotton waste or cleaning cloth having been drawn into the vacuum pipe system and causing intermittent or partial obstruction. Such cases do occur occasionally, and the wire cage inside the coupling is designed to prevent them.

There was also some rather indefinite evidence as to a noise like that caused by the sudden operation of the brake in the guard's van, at the last moment prior to the impact, which indicated the same possibility of temporary obstruction.

Tests were made, therefore, on the engine and tender by coupling another engine in rear of the tender and raising the vacuum thereon, afterwards admitting air in front so as to draw any loose obstruction to the coupling pipe, but without result; subsequently the whole of the vacuum piping, on the engine, tender, and coaches, was dismantled and thoroughly examined, but no obstruction could be found. In this connection it should be noted that the seven coaches form a set train which had not been uncoupled since 16 April.

At my Inquiry, Mr. E. S. Hunter, a passenger who was travelling in the last but one trailing compartment of the second coach immediately ahead of Pullman No 30, gave evidence to the effect that at two points on the journey the coach had been rocking and jolting in an altogether abnormal manner, and he suggested that some defect had developed in the bogie which might have affected the operation of the brake. At neither of the two points in question, which were in the neighbourhood of Three Bridges, and between Haywards Heath and Lewes, did he consider the speed very high, and he was quite confident that the speed at other points was much higher but that the abnormal motion was no longer noticeable.

Mr. Hunter stated that he 'was a frequent traveller on the line and was well acquainted with the ordinary discomfort of travelling in a coach coupled to a Pullman', but that the motion on this occasion was something quite different and led him to think that the bogie might have broken loose from the underframe.

An examination of the bogies, underframe, and vacuum piping and brake gear of the coach revealed no defect, and I am satisfied that this had no bearing on the origin of the accident. I discuss certain other points of Mr. Hunter's evidence below.

Conclusion.

An exhaustive examination having failed to indicate any defect in, or possible cause of failure of, the brake equipment, the only alternative explanation is faulty handling of the train by the driver.

Driver Suckling, after exercising all proper caution in reducing speed when approaching, thought that he might stop too soon and replaced the brake handle in the running position shortly before entering the station. I think it is probable that the action of the small ejector, supplemented by the crosshead vacuum pump which is fitted to this class of engine, restored the vacuum and released the brakes more rapidly than he realised, with the result that it required a fuller application than he expected to produce immediately the final retardation to a stop.

Driver Suckling was well acquainted with the train, the route, and the King Arthur class of engine. He had been working another type of engine on the previous day, fitted with the Westinghouse brake, but he is quite definite that the different class of engine and engine brake equipment had no bearing on the accident and that he would just as soon work with the vacuum as the Westinghouse. I do not see any reason to question his opinion on this point.

I conclude therefore that the cause of this accident was an error of judgment on the part of Driver Suckling in handling his brake when entering the platform.

He is a man of 59 years of age with 43 years' railway service, 29 years as driver. He has a good record. I am informed that he has been working in and out of congested areas for many years and is considered a very reliable and experienced driver.

Remarks.

As regards Mr. Hunter's remarks on the abnormal vibration and jolting of the trailing-end of the second coach in which he was riding, an examination of the bogie and frame of the coach made it clear that there was no breakage or defect which was likely to cause unusual risk of accident. It is a matter of common knowledge that vibration is most noticeable immediately above a bogie and in this case the stock was old and of a light type of construction, while the speed was high. As it happened, the track had been tested by a Hallade Recorder a few days before with results which were generally very satisfactory, but there is reverse curvature in the neighbourhood of Three Bridges, and I think it likely that the abnormal motion was due to periodic vibrations which happened to synchronise in such a manner as to reach an unusually acute peak. The buffing and drawgear in use between the second coach and the Pullman was of standard type, the central coupling (buck-eye) equipment at this end of the Pullman not being in use.

The collapse of the underframe of the trailing end of the second coach under the blow from the leading Pullman and other coaches in rear is a matter which calls for comment. Fortunately neither of the two underframes rose above the other, but the headstock of the second coach was driven in bodily a distance of about 15 ins, the side members and diagonals buckling sideways. The construction of the Pullman (dated 1922) was of the heavy type which is characteristic of these vehicles, whereas the coach ahead was 25 years old and of a very much lighter type, and it is hardly to be wondered that the whole violence of impact was concentrated at this one point with

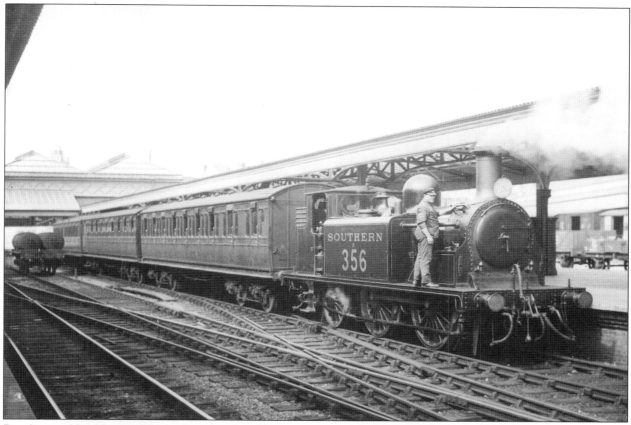

Despite considerable searching we have been unable to locate a view of the scene after the collision. Indeed this is also the nearest we can get to Platform 3 of the terminus; 'D1' 0-4-2T No 356, the former Coulsdon, awaiting departure in the Summer of 1925. It is seen here with the prefix 'B' above the letter indicating it originated from the Brighton section. ('A' was used for Ashford' and 'E' for Eastleigh'.) Subsequent renumbering saw it appear as No 2356. It would not survive into BR days and was withdrawn in May 1940 after a life just short of 54 years. *Transport Treasury*

comparatively little damage elsewhere.

In connection with other accident reports in the last few years, attention has been drawn to the desirability of homogeneous strength and design of underframes and of buffering throughout a train and there is no doubt that it would be much to be preferred that vehicles used with Pullmans should be of a heavier type than the one in question; the collision clearly illustrates the effects of the impact given by the Pullman and the rear portion of the train on a very light type of underframe.

I have therefore discussed with the Company's Officers the question of the use of old and light stock in conjunction with Pullmans in fast main line trains similar to the one in question. They are fully alive to the desirability of heavier stock and have given me details as to their policy and construction programme for the last five

years, showing that during this period very considerable progress has been made in the provision of heavy corridor bogie stock of an up-to-date type for main line services. For 1930 the normal programme has been increased by an additional 200 such coaches in connection with the remission of the Railway Passenger duty, and the provision of 275 new coaches for the Brighton Electrification now in hand will release a number of modern coaches for use elsewhere.

There are at present five services daily to and from Eastbourne on which Pullman cars are run, and of these two are already equipped with corridor stock. The Company expect to be able to provide stock of modern type and heavy construction on the remaining three services within the next six months, and they anticipate that within two years it will be possible to provide new corridor stock on all these services.

In all the circumstances, and having regard to the rolling stock situation of the constituent Companies at the time of grouping, I doubt if there is justification for serious criticism in regard to the age and construction of the coaches in use in this case.

I am, Sir, your obedient Servant............. ."

Bibliography: 'The Book of the King Arthur 4-6-0s', by Richard Derry, published by Irwell Press. (What else…!)

Above and opposite: Two further views of Eastbourne, again unrelated to the article and instead showing work in connection with electrification. Platform extensions are under way – Exmouth Junction concrete of course – whilst the former LBSCR signals are in the process of being replaced by standard SR upper quadrant fittings. *Rev A. Mace / Transport Treasury*

Stephen Townroe's Colour Archive

We are delighted to be able to continue with the colour archives of the late Stephen Townroe and with the theme of main line trains and the London Termini.

Should anyone not be familiar with the work of S. C. Townroe, suffice to say he was a professional railwayman who worked for the Southern Railway and subsequently British Railways Southern Region, rising through the ranks to be District Motive Power Superintendent at Eastleigh in the days of steam.

A committed steam man, he was also an enthusiast, relishing the chance to travel on the footplate when he could as well as taking several hundred quality images of the railway scene both on 'his patch' and beyond. His colour photography commenced prior to WW2 and although understandably limited at this time it also provides for a rare record. We intend to feature examples of these in a later issue. For now some images on the main lines out of London.

SCT206 One of the advantages of working on the railway was the access it gave. In his professional role he would have travelled around for official meetings and visits but which also gave the opportunity to find new vantage points for photography. Here is a typical example, just west of the flyover at Durnsford Road, as T9 No 30724 approaches on the down fast line with the 12.54pm Waterloo to Basingstoke service. The date is September 1954 although missing is the actual day and as no diaries survive we cannot be clear if this might even have been an official visit, perhaps to Woking or indeed the electric car sheds. In the far background is the SR's Durnsford Road power station and the electric depot. The lines on the extreme left of Durnsford Road are those of the District Line to Earls Court. The flyover here is where the up slow line crosses over the up and down fast lines so as to split the fast and slow lines into two parallel pairs from this point on through Earlsfield, Clapham Junction and on to Waterloo. No 30724 was a Basingstoke engine at this time, spending seven years working trains from the depot here from 1952 to 1959. It would move to Guildford in March 1959 and was withdrawn from there just two months later. (Copies of this and other S.C. Townroe colour images are available for private or commercial use. Please contact the Editor direct at the email address shown at the front of this issue.)

Image 48: SCT366 According to SCT, this was the first appearance of a rebuilt light pacific, No 34005 *Barnstaple*, at Waterloo in July 1957. It is also almost certainly an event SCT would have had prior knowledge of, the engine in sparkling condition and with the steam sanders in operation as well as steam to spare from the safety valves. Duty 252 – as per the route disc – was an Eastleigh turn working a Waterloo to Bournemouth West service; which also explains the carriage roof boards. SCT's records are usually 100% accurate although the limited details he provides here are slightly at odds with correspondents in the *Railway Observer*. What we can say for certain is that No 34005 was taken into Eastleigh Works on 14 May 1957 to emerge just six weeks later having received a general overhaul as well as being rebuilt as seen. This was after having covered some 489,808 recorded miles since new in 12 years. Tender No 3358 was similarly modified and attached, the pairing destined to remain together for the life of the engine. In this form *Barnstaple* would be in service until October 1965, running a further 347,524 miles.

Opposite: SCT650 A case of right place - right time. Blue liveried No 35024 *East Asiatic Company* leaving Waterloo in June 1949 on what is marked as a Special working; notice at least one pristine Pullman car in the formation. (The occasion was a Royal visit by the then Princess Elizabeth to Weymouth. One month earlier the engine had been officially named at Waterloo by HRH Prince Axel of Denmark, Chairman of the East Asiatic shipping line.) No 35024 remained in the attractive blue colour for just two years when it was repainted in standard green. As seen here it was noted that the BR emblem on the tender had also been hand painted. No 35024 was built to the third and final order for Merchant Navy Pacifics. Completed at Eastleigh in November 1948 it was in service until January 1965 and was probably withdrawn simply as being in need of repairs which at this late stage in the life of steam could not be justified. The previous recorded works visit for the engine had been a Light Intermediate repair in June/July 1963.

Above: SCT658 Away from the South Western lines for a change and instead we are near Brixton where 'C' class 0-6-0 No 31688 has charge of what appears to be a fitted freight. The view was taken in May 1954 at which time No 31688 was a Hither Green engine and seemingly too not far out of overhaul – no steam escaping from where it shouldn't. No 31668 had a useful life of nearly sixty years, built by Neilsen, Reid & Co for the South Eastern Railway and taken out of service by BR in February 1960.

Plenty more colour to come in future issues of
SOUTHERN TIMES
much of it previously unseen.

Opposite: SCT674 The combination of a black locomotive with crimson and cream passenger stock was almost as pleasing to the eye as a green train – others are permitted to disagree of course! On this occasion we see Schools No 30911 *Dover* at Petts Wood with probably a Hastings line service; Schools class engine and width restricted stock comprising Maunsell set No 478.

Above: SCT675 Reported as being a school special, appropriately hauled by another member of the Schools class, No 30915 *Brighton*. This was one of the class modified by Mr Bulleid with a multiple jet blastpipe and wider chimney which is generally said to have made an already very good engine better still. Once more this is near Brixton and so possibly taken on the same day as the 'C' class seen earlier. Maunsell coaching stock but this time seemingly a scratch formation.

SCT703 We are back on South Western lines again now, at Surbiton, as 'N15' No 30450 *Sir Kay* passes through non-stop on the 2.05pm Waterloo to Basingstoke and Salisbury working. Surbiton station had been rebuilt by the Southern Railway in the 1930s; all concrete and glass in contemporary style. At the time certainly fashionable even if a bit austere, it has come to be accepted as an example of a particular architectural style and is now much loved. The centre line on which the train is running is the down through line, the down slow being the platform road to the right whilst there is also a down loop platform used mainly by Hampton Court services. On the opposite side, the up fast and up slow lines run either side of the left hand island platform.

SCT716 Royal train duty for yet another Schools, No 30936 *Cranleigh*, about to pass through Battersea Park en-route to Epsom for the 1954 Derby. The white roof of the steam engine will be noted whilst this and the formation – Pullmans of course – have attracted the attention of lesser mortals in the EMU passing in the opposite direction. The engine would have been especially prepared at Stewarts Lane for the turn with a stand by in a similar state of readiness should it be necessary.

Opposite: SCT729 Workaday grime livery for No 34006 *Bude* as it enters Weybridge with the down 3.00pm Waterloo to Exeter train in 1955. This was a Nine Elms engine which also explains the external condition – boys prepared to work as cleaners as the first step towards a footplate career not easy to find in the London area at this time. BR Mk1 coaching stock appears dominant whilst from the signal it is not surprising a train is also due on the down slow line, such was the intensity of service on the Southern lines for most of the day. No 34006 would be destined to be one of the final original Bulleid Pacifics to survive, unique at that time in retaining its extra long smoke deflectors. It was withdrawn in in March 1967.

Above: SCT805 Despite its plethora of home grown Pacifics, the Southern also played host to a few examples of the new BR Standard Britannia class in the early 1950s, including No 70004 *William Shakespeare*. After a period at Nine Elms the engine moved to Stewarts Lane where it too was a regular performer on the prestige Golden Arrow, seen here with the down train at Sevenoaks in September 1954 - whistle chiming. Whether these engines were actually needed on the Southern is a mute point, notwithstanding the unreliability of the Bulleid type, there were so many Bulleids that failures in service could usually be covered. Probably the reason was to give as many depots and crews some familiarity with the Standard designs, the Class 5, Class 4 tender types and Class 4, 3 and 2 tank designs destined to be seen regularly on Southern services from the early to mid-1950s onwards.

SCT838 The down Bournemouth Belle Pullman at Clapham Junction in the early 1950s passing Clapham A signal box – the one that collapsed some years later. In charge is No 35018 *British India Line* in blue livery and destined later to be the first member of the class to be rebuilt. Assuming the train to be running to schedule, the time would be soon after 12.30pm, the latter the departure time from Waterloo, whilst on board stewards would be going around inviting passengers to partake of lunch – after all what was the point of travelling Pullman otherwise?

Inset: SCT840 To conclude this instalment of colour, we have newly rebuilt No 35020 *Bibby Line* passing Brookwood on a down West of England working in June 1956. This time the 'blood and custard' stock appear to be mostly of Bulleid design, the profile of which seems to match the curvature of the tender. On the up slow line is a suburban EMU, probably a SUB set, whilst above the rails are some of the LSWR lower quadrant pneumatic signals. No 35020 was one of several of the class withdrawn in 1965, the scale of withdrawals at that time leaving the Southern Region short of steam stock on occasions.

David McKenna
Chairman and General Manager, Southern Region 1963 – 1968

As is well known and need not be recounted in detail here, the implementation of the Bournemouth electrification in July 1967 witnessed the final end of steam on the Western section of the Southern Region, the Central and Eastern sections having gone over completely to electric and diesel power beforehand.

Not unnaturally the Southern Region management were keen to promote the modernisation of their railway and whilst the public relations department (sic) would send out posters extolling patience as necessary while engineering work was undertaken, there was one face that appeared on several of these to extoll the benefits of what was to come. That face was of the General Manager, David McKenna.* (The new trains might perhaps not have been quite what might have been expected especially when compared with stock already running elsewhere on the BR network. Draughty REP and TC sets that rattled and banged through stations creating pressure waves totally alien to what passengers might have experienced before. Woebetide anyone who attempted to partake of a drink at places like Hampton Court Junction, the up through line at Farnborough and through Worting Junction! Regular travellers would learn fast.)

Any such disadvantages were outweighed by the faster and regular interval services that now existed, exactly the prophecy of the SR General Manager, David McKenna. Unfortunately the new timetable did not always run as planned, a fact which would later have an effect upon his own career path.

McKenna was a career railwayman through and through. Mild in manner and meticulous in practice, David McKenna pursued two great passions in life: public transport and music.

Born at the Admiralty, in London, he was one of two sons of the Liberal MP Reginald McKenna, who, between 1908 and 1916, was successively First Lord of the Admiralty, Home Secretary and then Chancellor of the Exchequer under Herbert Asquith. David shared his father's attitude to efficiency and numeracy but shunned a career either in the armed forces or politics. He was educated at Eton - where he was captain (or head boy) - and then went up to Trinity College, Cambridge, obtaining first class honours in mathematics and engineering. (David's brother Michael died in 1931.)

His transport career commenced with the nascent London Passenger Transport Board where its vice chairman, Frank Pick, became one of his main influences in considering transport and its widest social and environmental significance. At the LPTB he was occupied in the actuary, staff, development superintendent's, and chairman's offices, being appointed one of the vice-chairman's assistants in late 1936.

In this area he wrestled with the problems of London's railways; in subsequent years going on to the problems of the whole country. Outside of the office his relaxation was the promotion of Baroque music, particularly that of Bach, which he also performed as an accomplished singer and harpsichordist. An important milestone also occurred in 1934 when he married the Lady Cecilia Keppel, daughter of the 9th Earl of Albemarle. They would have three daughters during a marriage that lasted some 68 years.

On the outbreak of the Second World War, he was commissioned, not unnaturally, in the Transportation Branch of the Royal Engineers and served in Iraq, Turkey, India and Burma, reaching the rank of Lieutenant Colonel. These services were recognised with an MBE in 1943 and later an OBE in 1946. (He was subsequently made CBE in 1967.)

He played a large part in the postwar organisation of London's railways following nationalisation in 1948; when the LPTB had become London Transport. He effectively drafted the 1949 transport white paper, whose proposals included track widenings, electrification of surface lines, and 103 miles of new deep-level tunnels under London. One of these proposals would later manifest as the Victoria line opened between 1968 and 1971,

David McKenna *CBE, MA, MinstT 1911-2003.* Chairman and General manager, British Railways Southern Region 1963-1968. *British Railways*

although this had ended at Brixton, rather than, as once planned, East Croydon.

He served as Assistant General Manager of the Southern Region from 1955 to 1961 and was promoted to the first combined role of General Manager and Chairman of the SR in 1963. In this role he had total autonomy and it was only after sustained pressure from above that he reluctantly accepted the need for Assistant General Managers to cover movement and commercial operations – and then took a year to appoint them! Prior to moving to Waterloo, the intervening 12 months, from 1 January to 31 December 1962, saw him as Chief Commercial Officer at the BRB working with Dr Beeching on the reshaping of the network.

The Southern was BR's largest and most important network for dealing with the capital and its harassed commuters, to whose exasperation McKenna unfortunately contributed when, in July 1967, he instituted his radical timetable. This envisaged a level of punctuality the system could not deliver and changes were quickly implemented. His success though in seeing through the

Bournemouth electrification did at least appease most commuters on the lines out of Waterloo.

David McKenna left the Southern Region on 1 June 1968 upon promotion to the Board of British Railways as a full time member. This might have come earlier but it was vetoed by the Rt Hon Barbara Castle MP, then Minister of Transport in the Labour Government of the time. Quoting T. R. Gourvish from his 'British Railways 1948-73. A business history',** '....she believed it to be politically inexpedient to promote the manager of a region suffering adverse publicity after problems with its 1967 timetable and a serious accident at Hither Green (3 November 1967). He should, she said, "sweat out the problems of the Southern."'

Whilst at Waterloo he had to deal with the issues surrounding potential closure of the Ashford-Ore-Hastings (subsequently reprieved and continuing to operate today), and Alton-Winchester lines. As at King's Cross where his Eastern Region colleague Gerard Fiennes had been able to extract concessions on proposed closures so too was McKenna but only in relation to the first named Southern line. Speaking of Alton-Winchester, Gourish quotes him in June 1967 as informing the BRB, he was 'unable to make an economic case for the closure of Alton-Winchester'. The figures quoted by the BRB in the 'Reshaping' report indicated a net saving of £20,900 could be achieved but McKenna considered these, 'a very misleading basis for action'. The Alton-Winchester closure proposal would drag on for some years to come with allegations from the BRB that the Southern (and the Eastern with their own specific examples) were simply trying to protect their existing level of operation. Countering this were widespread allegations that BR had allowed the service to deteriorate. Alton-Winchester would eventually close in February 1973.

Somewhat ironically considering the last paragraph, McKenna subsequently served on the BR Board with responsibility for the passenger side of the business although any further dealings or comments he may have made relative to this closure are not reported. He remained a full time member until 1976 after which he was then part time for a further two years, finally leaving in August 1978. He commented that he saw his Board role as the pinnacle of his career and had even had his name put forward for the role of Chief Executive at one point. Even after leaving railway service, it could hardly be called retirement, he continued to be devoted to the cause of public transport and would later be outspoken in his comments on what he described as a '… bungled privatisation and subsequent mismanagement.'

McKenna also served as Chairman of British Transport Advertising from 1968 to 1981. Member of the Dover Harbour Board, 1969 to 1980, and Director, Isles of Scilly Steamship Co., 1976 to 1992. He was a great proponent of cross channel transport and the later Channel Tunnel. This support led to another honour, that of Commandeur de l'Ordre National du Mérite in 1974. (Previous recognition of his belief in cross channel co-operation had been in September 1967 when, during a ceremony at Boulogne to view the site for the SRN4 cross-channel hovercraft terminal then under construction, he was made an honorary citizen of the French town by Senator Mayor M. Henneguelle.) Away from railways and transport, other posts included being Chairman of the governors at Sadler's Wells, 1962-76, Chairman of the Bach Choir, 1964-76, and fellow and vice-president of the Royal College of Music.

He retired to Cornwall where, despite a stroke in 1995 which affected his physical abilities, he continued to be mentally active assisting researchers in their studies of his great aunt Gertrude Jekyll, the garden designer, as well as the writer Martin Farr who would subsequently compile a biography of his father Reginald McKenna.

*To be strictly accurate, electrification to Bournemouth had first been publicly mooted by various senior Southern Region managers including Charles Hopkins at the formal opening of the Hither Green Continental Freight Depot in October 1960. Even so it would not be until late 1964 that formal approval was given to the scheme by the British Railways Board.

** 'British Railways 1948-73. A Business History'. By T. R. Gourvish, Cambridge University Press 1986.

Off the beaten track for a moment and a wonderful use for a signal away from the railway. The location is Fishbourne and the point of embarkation for the car ferry from the Isle of Wight to Portsmouth. There appears to be an operating control, of sorts, on the post, but whether it was still being used as an indication to embark is not known. *Rev A. Mace / Transport Treasury.*

Off the beaten track:
Southern Pacifics at Birmingham Snow Hill

Saturday 27 April 1963 was a red-letter day for spotters and enthusiasts in the Birmingham area when no less than 15 special trains were run in the morning carrying Southampton football supporters to Birmingham Snow Hill for their club's F A Cup match with Manchester United being played at Villa Park - the home ground of local team Aston Villa. (Southampton lost '1-0'.)

Twelve of the Southern engines involved were Nos 34009 *Lyme Regis*, 34028 *Eddystone*, 34039 *Boscastle*, 34040 *Crewkerne*, 34042 *Dorchester,* 34045 *Ottery St. Mary*, 34046 *Braunton*, 34050 *Royal Observer Corps,* 34052 *Lord Dowding*, 34088 *213 Squadron*, 34094 *Mortehoe* and 34098 *Templecombe*. Three of the trains took the 'Old Worse and Worse' line (the Worcester route north of Oxford) to reach Birmingham Snow Hill via Stourbridge Junction. These services were hauled by Nos 34009, 34039 and 34046, with each also being piloted by an LMS '8F', respectively Nos 48417, 48478 and 48430. At least one WR engine was similarly involved with a train which had originated on the Southern, No 7919 *Runter Hall,* but it is not clear if this engine had worked through from the south or had taken over at some point en-route. Those services not taking the Worcester line continued north via Banbury and Leamington. Presumably all the engines were serviced at Tyseley with the same Southern engines being used for the return workings, in all cases with a pilotman on board. By comparison, Manchester United had just six special trains running south. (No 34094 *Mortehoe* was in action away from home territory the following month when on 12 May it visited Doncaster on a special starting from Birmingham New Street and organised by the Warwickshire Railway Society.) The images show three of the Southern engines at Snow Hill as well as an LMS 8F unusually seen carrying 'Class A' headlamps. *Rev A. Mace / Transport Treasury.*

Not to be forgotten of course were the electric services operated by the Southern. These had commenced on both the LSWR and LBSCR prior to Grouping and expanded what we now know of as the third-rail network in subsequent decades.

Above: On the switchback and curving 'Portsmouth Direct', '4COR' No 3125 is seen between Liphook and Liss with a Portsmouth semi-fast, 23 June 1950. *R. E. Vincent / Transport Treasury*

Opposite top: No date this time, but the location is undeniably Clapham Junction. '2BIL' No 2032 heading what is probably a Waterloo – Alton service although it should be noted this same headcode was also used for race-day specials between Waterloo and Esher. *R. E. Vincent / Transport Treasury*

Opposite bottom: Again a location that is easily referenced, Chelsfield. Leading this service is a former '3SUB' augmented to a four-car unit with the addition of an additional (wider) trailer. The inverted 'Λ' symbol was used for services on one of four routes: Cannon St - Sevenoaks via Petts Wood (not Lewisham), Charing Cross - Sevenoaks via Petts Wood (not Lewisham), Holborn Viaduct - Gillingham via Herne Hill, and Victoria - Gillingham via Herne Hill. *R. E. Vincent / Transport Treasury*

Above: This time we have a later '4SUB' unit, No 4647, having just left Knockholt tunnel, no confirmed date but likely around May 1952. The service is between Charing Cross and Sevenoaks. *R. E. Vincent / Transport Treasury*

Opposite top: Another '4COR' set but this time on a Mid-Sussex line service near Holmwood, 3 May 1953. *R. E. Vincent / Transport Treasury*

Opposite bottom: At the same location on the same day, this time No 3107. *R. E. Vincent / Transport Treasury*

Look out for Issue 2 of Southern Times available in June 2022.

Please contact The Transport Treasury for details.

Opposite: Hopefully a reader with knowledge of this specific area can assist here with a location – certainly a regular stabling point as witness the walkway at solebar level. Early BR days with the 'S' prefix. *R. E. Vincent / Transport Treasury*

Top: This is a '6PUL' unit (Pullman car as part of the formation). The photographer states the location to be 'Reigate ?' but that is certainly incorrect as the train is on the Brighton main line. *R. E. Vincent / Transport Treasury*

Bottom: Finally in this section, another '6PUL' at Croydon on 23 March 1950. The firm of Messrs Hall & Co. in the background referred to an expansive company who had interests in coal at a number of stations in Surrey and Sussex. *R. E. Vincent / Transport Treasury*

Guildford and Waterloo via Main Line A Passenger's Description of the First Electric Journey

The February 1937 issue of the *Southern Railway Magazine* carried on pages 42/43 a short article on on the above contributed by F E Box.

Although entitled 'A Passenger's Description', the accuracy of the information especially appertaining to speeds does raise the question whether there might not have been some official backing to the record.

'F E Box', or more accurately, Frank Box, was a renowned enthusiast and photographer and whilst the article was illustarted with three images we do not feel the quality of these are suitable for reproduction. (The collection of material taken by Frank, and later his son Donovan Box, are in the care of the National Railway Museum.)

"A few minutes after sunrise on Sunday 3 January, an eight-coach train, bearing the new headcode '7', and comprising four new two-coach units, Nos 1915, 1909, 1911 and 1914 'backed', if this term is properly applicable to electric stock whose 'head' and 'tail' are interchangeable, into platform 5 at Guildford to the form the 8.30am up.

This was the first electric train from Guildford via Woking, available for passengers, although experimental running had been in progress since 1 December.

When booking for the journey, I expected no record of other than sentimental interest to result, as no drastic revision had been made in the old 'steam' timing, and presumably the electric trains will be gradually introduced and run in on the old schedules until the complete changeover is made.

There were but few passengers, and those mostly railway servants, who joined the train at Guildford, bu the presence of Mr Bridger the station master, seemed to add a little touch of kindly and quiet dignity to an otherwise unobtrusive 'send-off', which, however much lacking in ceremony, was at all events marked by commendable and precise punctuality.

The running throughout , as anticipated, was restrained,whilst each stop was carefully made; generally the maximum speed between stations was almost 45 to 47 mph, exceptionally 57.7 mph was obtained down the 1 in 111 before Worplesdon, but the rate of 50 mph was not again reached until beyond the seventh mile-post when speed rose to 51.7 mph.

The train was kept 4½ minutes at Woking and held nearly 5 minutes at Weybridge, awaiting the Chertsey line connection.; A very caution entry into Surbiton station - where engineering works were in progress , and the new up local platform was being used - was followed by a careful crossing from 'local' to the 'through' line. Nevertheless as the train ran into Waterloo the minute hand of 'Big Ben' was pointing exactly to the half-hour, and the actual stop was made at 9hr, 30 mins. 27 sec am., Virtually on time.

The same units formed the first public down train at 10.12am, Nos 1914 and 1911 returning to Guildford, but Nos 1919 and 1915 were detached at Woking for Aldershot.

Once again the running was sedate, 55.9 mph sustained between mileposts eight and nine, being the maximum. The through line was followed to Hampton Court Junction, two signal stops of very short duration were encountered before Surbiton, and 3½ minutes were spent at Weybridge, but yet the Woking arrival was no less than 3½ minutes early.

Slight and excessive delay, due to the new and stiff couplings, was caused by the detachment of the Aldershot units, and the Woking departure was 1½ minutes late, but this was easily retrieved on the liberal schedule thence. With a steady 43 to 45 mph up the bank from Worplesdon, Guildford was reached 1½ minutes early at 11hr 20mins 34sec. am."

Copnor Level Crossing 1908

A chance comment and who knows what can result, often something not previously considered. Such was the case with this image of the signal box at what was then known as 'COPNOR CROSSING' dated (from the negative packet) as being from 1908. The signal box itself is from 1879 and was of Saxby & Farmer design. (An earlier box, possibly a simple level crossing box known as COPNOR GATES had existed prior to this date.)

Copnor Crossing was on the line between Fratton East to the south and Green Lanes to the north; part of the Cosham, Portcreek Junction and Portsmouth Joint Line. Joint in so far as it was jointly worked between the LBSCR and LSWR with receipts being pooled.

As the name implies, the signal box here, standing on the east side of the main line, existed primarily to control the road level crossing which even in what were the early years of the 20th century was a busy thoroughfare for road traffic.

At an educated guess, based on the lack of any obvious rodding other than for the gate locks, this was a hand operated crossing which meant the signalman would also have been kept busy. Clearly posed - notice the child just getting into shot on the road side of the gates - are we to assume it may even have been double manned during peak rail/ road times?

Resultant road congestion was instrumental in the provision of a bridge to replace the crossing c1918 subsequent to which the name was changed to that of 'COPNOR INTERMEDIATE' having just up and down signals in either direction and just four operating levers left in the frame; Nos 1 and 2 for up line signals, and 9 and 10 for the down line, all other levers being spare. COPNOR INTERMEDIATE closed in 1935.

With grateful thanks to Chris Richardson for permission to reproduce the image.

Southern Railway Meritorious Service Medal

In 1940 the Southern Railway created the special war medal to be awarded to members of staff for deeds of outstanding merit performed in connection with the war.

The medals are made of silver guilt and take the form of a locomotive driving wheel with laurel wreath superimposed. The cross is an early form of the Victoria Cross with the letters SR in the centre. The ribbon looks like a railway track in the Southern Railway colours of green and gold. The ribbon attachment mimics a vehicle spring.

Eighteen of these were presented at a ceremony held at Waterloo on August 18th 1940. The Bluebell Museum has on display the medal awarded to Dock Gateman Esmond Roote. Esmond and four others launched a boat when a mine entered Folkestone Harbour and drifted towards the viaduct and swing bridge. They threw a line over the mine and secured it to a buoy.

The Southern Railway Magazine devoted over three pages of the September 1940 issue to details of the awards and recipients.

The Southern Railway files for these medals are at the National Archives at Kew. These records show that a second batch of medals were to be presented. However, there is no details at the PRO of them being presented. Also, there is no reference in the Southern Railway Magazine to a second batch being presented.

Towards the end of 2021 an ex-railwayman got in touch with the Museum offering to donate a selection of badges. One of the badges was, in fact, a meritorious medal for George Henry Leach. Also, the donation included the handwritten dedication on special note paper detailing the heroic act. .

Lengthman George Henry Leach

"On the night of 22nd/23rd August 1940, George Henry Leach after cycling from his home at Aldershot, assisted in the isolation of burning wagons in an ammunition train which had been hit by a number of incendiary high explosive bombs whilst standing in the salvage sidings at Tongham, Surrey.

During the whole of the time the movement of wagons from the danger area was being made – approximate two hours – explosions were taking place, and Leach displayed courage and resource in carrying out the operations, which involved great personal risk."

George Leach's medal was in the second batch. The donor found the medal, among others, in a drawer in a Waterloo office during the rebuilding for the Channel Tunnel. He was given it and told that they were never presented as the Government told the Southern Railway that presenting such medals was inappropriate during wartime. Whether that is true or not for some reason the medals were not presented.

Further research shows that George worked with George Frederick Keen a Ganger to save the wagons. The London Gazette for 15th November 1940 states that both men were awarded the George Medal for bravery.

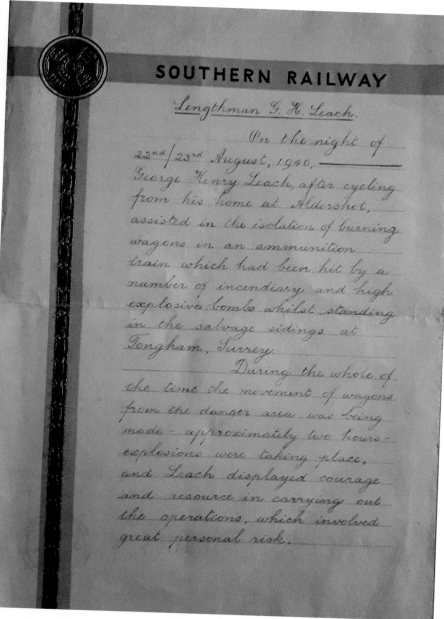

George Keen's medal is on display in the National Railway Museum, perhaps it too came from a drawer at Waterloo.

Editors note: 'Treasures from the Bluebell Railway Museum' is intended to be a regular series in Southern Times, kindly compiled by Assistant Curator Tony Hillman.

The Bluebell Railway Museum, located on Platform 2 at Sheffield Park, is well worth a visit and is a veritable treasure trove of artefacts and ephemera from the Southern Railway and its constituents. We look forward to featuring more treasures in the next issue.

From the footplate

'From the footplate' is the forum for you to have your say.

Discussion comment (correction) on topics in this and later on in subsequent issues, additional information and even ideas for topics you would like to see covered.

We have a few writing friends who are sometimes prepared to take up the challenge. However if you too would like to submit material, written or illustrative we would be pleased to receive it.

Book reviews (restricted to Southern related subjects) is something else we might hopefully feature; so do have a word with your publisher's marketing department. (So far as book reviews are concerned we will always contact the writer to advise him of our review prior to it going to print.)

The usual caveats as regards letters will apply, in so much that the views of the writer are not necessarily those of the Publisher and / or Editor and that the Publisher / Editor reserve the right to shorten, conclude or decline to publish correspondence if necessary.

We conclude with an email already received from Nick Stanbury. Nick wrote principally in connection with a piece that had been published elsewhere but added an interesting caveat, 'I wonder if I might be able to produce a 'guest editorial' that would be of sufficient interest. Maybe something 'along the lines' (pun intended) of what prompted my interest in railways, and the Southern in particular…. .'.

Short answer, 'Absolutely, yes'. Guest editorials are very welcome; your chance to sound off too if you like but please do keep it relevant to the theme of 'Southern Times' and if possible within the remit of coverage.

We look forward to hearing from you.

No 34021 *Dartmoor* makes a spirited departure from Waterloo in April 1965 with what is described (from the headcode) as a Southampton Terminus working. Might this have been the only time the painter was captured in this particular task? *Graham Smith courtesy Richard Sissons*